TOLD YOU SO

MAYCI NEELEY

SIMON & SCHUSTER
New York   Amsterdam/Antwerp   London
Toronto   Sydney/Melbourne   New Delhi

Simon & Schuster
1230 Avenue of the Americas
New York, NY 10020

For more than 100 years, Simon & Schuster has championed authors and the stories they create. By respecting the copyright of an author's intellectual property, you enable Simon & Schuster and the author to continue publishing exceptional books for years to come. We thank you for supporting the author's copyright by purchasing an authorized edition of this book.

No amount of this book may be reproduced or stored in any format, nor may it be uploaded to any website, database, language-learning model, or other repository, retrieval, or artificial intelligence system without express permission. All rights reserved. Inquiries may be directed to Simon & Schuster, 1230 Avenue of the Americas, New York, NY 10020 or permissions@simonandschuster.com.

Copyright © 2025 by Mayci J, LLC

All rights reserved, including the right to reproduce this book or portions thereof in any form whatsoever. For information, address Simon & Schuster Subsidiary Rights Department, 1230 Avenue of the Americas, New York, NY 10020.

First Simon & Schuster hardcover edition October 2025

SIMON & SCHUSTER and colophon are registered trademarks of Simon & Schuster, LLC

Simon & Schuster strongly believes in freedom of expression and stands against censorship in all its forms. For more information, visit BooksBelong.com.

Interior design by Wendy Blum

Manufactured in the United States of America

ISBN 978-1-6680-9992-6

AUTHOR'S NOTE

The events in this book concern real people, including children. Some names, places, and identifiable details have been changed. Additionally, I've reconstructed dialogue, to the best of my ability, using a combination of diary entries, text messages, DMs, and conversations with people who were involved.

For Hudson, my Saving Grace

TOLD YOU SO

ONE

THE DAY MY BOYFRIEND DIES, HE TEXTS ME TO SAY HE'S sorry. He loves me. He'll never forgive himself for hurting me while I'm pregnant with his baby.

Arik's text ends with a typo. A single letter *J*. I don't understand why he hasn't finished his thought until my mom takes me out to lunch that afternoon. While scrolling Instagram at our usual table, I see a picture of Arik on my timeline with the caption "R.I.P." He's crashed his car while texting me.

That night, three hundred people follow me on Instagram. Hunched over my phone on my parents' couch, I scroll past dozens of posts about Arik: pictures of him playing baseball, grinning at the camera, laughing with his family. There are screenshots of news stories about the crash that killed him, photos of people sobbing, and broken-heart emojis, all mixed in with the usual Instagram content—blurry selfies, food porn, a mediocre sunset. Those happy photos feel like they've been posted from another universe. Reminders of a time before I got pregnant and had to move back in with my Mormon parents in Southern California. Before I had to leave my scholarship and Division 1 tennis career at Brigham Young University behind.

I feel like I have to post something. But I have no idea what to write. I don't want to admit that hours before Arik died, I'd learned he cheated on me. Devastated, I'd said the cruelest things I could think of: that he wouldn't meet his baby unless it was in court; that he would never see me again; that I would never forgive him.

How could I explain via Instagram what it felt like to learn—at that dingy restaurant with my mom—that Arik died while texting me to ask for forgiveness, to tell me that I deserved better, to say that he loved me? How do you write a post about that?

WHEN YOU'RE FOURTEEN WEEKS pregnant and your boyfriend dies, people say a lot of things. "You'll meet someone else. You're still young." "You have plenty of time to find a father for your baby." "You don't look that sad in the pictures you post on Instagram." "God has a plan for you." I've known all along that God has a plan for everyone. I just don't know why mine is so shitty.

By twenty, I've already been drugged and raped. I've escaped an abusive relationship, only to fall in love with someone amazing and get pregnant unexpectedly. The night Arik dies, my mom is so worried about me that she drags an extra mattress into her bedroom so she can keep an eye on me while I sleeplessly stare at the ceiling.

THE NEXT SEVEN MONTHS are a gray, depressive blur. The easiest tasks—getting up, eating breakfast, taking the online classes that will allow me to keep my NCAA tennis eligibility—feel impossible. More than once, I think about dying.

You wouldn't know it from my Instagram feed. I don't post any shots of me sobbing to sad music in the shower or writing that I want to die in my journal. Instead, I upload pictures of me holding a starfish to obscure my massive belly. And another of me smiling on a cruise ship, pretending I'm not thinking about jumping overboard.

When I look back on that twenty-year-old gripping the railing and debating drowning herself in the ocean, I want to tell her that things will get better. That she'll forgive herself. That even though this pregnancy is unexpected, she'll love her baby more than anything in the world and fight hard for her next ones.

TOLD YOU SO

I want to tell her that she'll fall in love again, in a big, beautiful, dramatic way, that she'll learn to live her life without fear of judgment, and that at some point she'll hear the phrase "soft swinging" and not only know what it means but understand it's the scandal that brings her to reality TV.

Most of all, I want to tell her that the tragedies and trauma she's experienced won't define her. That there's no reason to feel shame about any of her mistakes—that the only shame is in hiding them.

TWO

I GREW UP MORMON, WHICH MEANS I GREW UP GOING TO Mormon dance parties. These are like other dance parties, except they're held in church buildings, and sometimes people pray before stepping onto a basketball court and dancing to "Don't Stop Believin'."

I ring in 2010 at the Aliso Viejo New Year's Dance with my friend and tennis teammate Cassidy, who's Christian but not Mormon. Cassidy is small and blond and loves to have a good time. She and I are dancing to a clean version of a Black-Eyed Peas song when Cole—who I've heard through the grapevine is eighteen—comes over to us. It's almost midnight, which means he's looking for someone to kiss.

My blond hair, burnt stick-straight, clings to the back of my neck. My eyeliner, drawn on too heavy, runs down my cheeks. Cole is cute, but he's too old for me. Rumor has it he's already finished his first semester of college.

When the DJ starts a slow song, Cole asks me to dance. There's no way I'm slow dancing with an eighteen-year-old who might try to kiss me at midnight. Mormons aren't supposed to date until we're sixteen, and I don't bend rules, even though I'll be sixteen in two and a half months. So I tell Cole we can do a group dance, and that's how Cassidy, Cole, and I celebrate 2010.

IN UTAH, THERE ARE so many Mormons that the people you go to church with usually live on your block. It's different in California. There aren't any Mormons on our street. But because of our church's programming, I feel like I know every Mormon boy in Southern California. When it's time for my high school's winter formal, I consider the boys I've met at church dances, then use Facebook Messenger to invite Cole's cousin Mark to be my date. Mark and I don't really know each other, but I think he's cute. And I like that he's standoffish. It feels like there's some mystery there.

The night of the formal, Mark is forty-five minutes late to pick me up. I have to take photos in the front yard by myself. I'm confident enough that this doesn't bother me. But my parents think Mark is being disrespectful. My mom, hair blown-out, makeup perfect, keeps checking her watch. My dad, who's bald, mutters about my taste in boys under his breath.

When Mark gets to my house, Cole is with him. I don't know why he's not back at college. Maybe he's in trouble. I've heard he drinks and uses drugs. I'm not a rule-breaker, but I've always been intrigued by things that are off-limits—in part because I've never been told the reasoning behind a lot of Mormon rules. Why is a girl who has sex outside of marriage considered a slut when a guy can get away with it? Why can't Mormons drink coffee when it's made from beans but soda is OK when it's artificial?

Mark, Cole, and I take pictures in front of my parents' house, then go to a friend's for dinner. Afterward, we take a party bus to the formal, which is at the Nixon Library. It looks like something straight out of a wedding, with chandeliers and a fog machine. All night, I can't help but think that Cole is more fun to talk to than Mark. He's witty and exciting: a bad boy. Mark is quiet and a little sick. He keeps getting bloody noses, which grosses me out. But I still think I want him to be my first kiss.

I MAKE IT HAPPEN a few weeks later at my friend Taylor's sweet sixteen. Her dad owns the Grove, so that's where the party is. Mark and I spend the whole night grinding on the dance floor. At ten, I have to leave because I have a tennis match the next day. Tennis always takes priority: even over church.

Our family rule is that it's OK to play tournaments on Sundays, but not practice, because Mormons are technically supposed to keep the Sabbath day holy. Ideally, I wouldn't play at all on Sundays, but most tennis tournaments are on the weekends, and I need to play tournaments to be recruited to a D1 program like UCLA or BYU.

I appreciate that my parents understand this. They're religious, but not crazy devout. My dad's attitude is to bend the rules but not break them. He says he lives his life in line with God and Jesus, and if he gets to heaven and learns the Mormons weren't right, at least he'll have lived in a good and moral way. I like that. It leaves some gray area. I'm the only Mormon girl I know who wears bikinis and tube tops.

Before I leave the Grove, I wind my arms around Mark's neck and peck him a few times. When I pull back, he looks slightly disappointed, like he wanted more.

But I'm giddy. I've had my first kiss.

I'M THE BABY OF the family. Everyone else is out of the house by the time I'm a teenager, so it's up to me to keep my mom company. She's like the Mormon Kris Jenner—she hates missing out. If she weren't Mormon, she'd be the type of parent to let teenagers drink in her house. She likes when I have my friends over so she can keep an eye on us. She doesn't need to. I don't drink, swear, or smoke. I play tennis, and I go to church dances, and when those end early, I go to McDonald's or Del Taco.

But my sweet sixteen is different. I post the party on Facebook as an open invite, and hundreds of people show up, including teenagers I've never seen in my life. The party is "candy shop" themed, so there's candy everywhere: oversized multicolored lollipops and bowls of licorice and chocolate. Dozens of people I don't know show up at my house. Mark is mad at me for only pecking him at Taylor's birthday, so he spends the night dodging me. I try to dance with him a few times, but it goes nowhere.

It's turning into a bad night for me, especially when some guy from a different high school shows up and pulls a knife on another kid—then threatens my parents. My dad's in the kitchen with my mom and my oldest sister Lauren, who's come into town from Utah for my party. He asks her to get a weapon. She says all we have are tennis rackets.

"Get a baseball bat," my dad says.

I'm in over my head. People are smoking in my parents' backyard and passing around Gatorade bottles filled with alcohol. Someone's getting arrested. I'm walking up to people I've never met and saying, "Stop, you can't do that." And "Please don't smoke here." And Mark—who was my first kiss, who I have a crush on—is making out with a random girl under the gazebo in the middle of the yard.

THREE

I'M COMPETITIVE, SO AFTER MARK BREAKS MY SIXTEEN-YEAR-old heart, I decide to win him back. I like the game of it. My sisters have taught me how to toy with guys, and I learn I have power over some of them. I start to make this one guy from my ward pick me up and take me to Taco Bell. And at a party a couple months after my birthday, I make out with Mark. It's a triumph. I'm not a person who likes to talk about feelings, so I enjoy not knowing what he's thinking all the time. I like that he plays hard to get. I like that I can get him anyway.

Mark and I hang out for a year. It isn't serious, but I spend a lot of time with him and his cousins, including Cole. As I get more confident, I flirt with them both. I like making them jealous.

My parents don't like Cole. My dad thinks he has a shady past. They don't like that he hasn't gone on mission, and they really don't like that he's older. At some point that summer, his parents send him to rehab, and he disappears for a couple months, which is confusing.

I'm a Goody Two-shoes, but when Cole gets back, I like that he tells me about drinking and doing drugs. I'm more intrigued by partying than sex at this point. I've learned about chastity, modesty, and the words of wisdom since I was little, but I'm still struggling to understand the why.

When things between Mark and me fizzle out, Cole and I start hanging out more. We hold hands but never kiss. I'm a prude. And I think the age gap makes it scary for him, too, but in the summer of 2012, when it's drizzling in Southern California, we kiss for the first time in my parents' driveway. It feels substantial. Real. We still never say we're together, and we keep our relationship a secret from my parents, but my siblings know. They think Cole is fun. And they're OK with us spending time together as long as we don't do anything besides kissing.

I LIKE COLE IN a way I never liked Mark. He makes me laugh. And he's different since he got out of rehab. He's a rule-follower. He's gone vegan. He's trying to get his life on track so he can go on mission.

It takes a year to return to good standing in the church after you've had premarital sex. It only takes a few months of repenting to come back from drinking or doing drugs.

Cole has done everything, so he has to go through a whole repentance process to get into a spiritual place where the church wants to send him out. We don't talk about it a lot, but I know it's important to him.

My sister McCall says she'll never marry a guy if he doesn't go on mission. Lots of Mormon girls feel like that. They won't date guys who don't go on mission or who come home early. I don't care if a guy has gone on mission. I just care that he has good character. The judgment around all of the Mormon rules seems so wrong to me. Cole and I don't talk about shame a lot, but his is right there, under the surface. There's so much pressure to be perfect when you're Mormon. Everything is black and white.

THE FIRST TIME I have an intense make-out session with Cole, my parents are out of town. When I go to the bathroom afterward, I realize my underwear is wet. I think there's something really wrong with me, like maybe I'm dying. Nobody has ever told me what being wet is. They haven't told me that I go a little heavy on the eyeliner or that Forever 21 neon crop tops aren't a great look on me either, but this is different. I feel scared. I know so little about my body and the world. Cole senses my innocence.

He never pressures me to do anything. He almost does the opposite. He takes care of me. He wants to make sure I make good choices. I can tell he really loves me. I think I might love him, too, but college is looming on the horizon.

I START THE TENNIS recruitment process. I'm a blue-chip recruit, which means I can basically go to any top-20 college. This isn't me being cocky. It's just true.

I can't decide between UCLA or BYU. I love the UCLA colors. And the school feels classy. It's fun to visit my middle sister McCall on campus and go shopping in Brentwood. But BYU is classic, and my oldest sister Lauren has become the new head coach there.

At one of McCall's UCLA matches, her coach comes up to me in the stands and asks, "Can I sit next to a future UCLA recruit?"

I tell him point-blank, "I'm going to BYU."

My mom laughs. UCLA is ranked in the top ten. BYU isn't even on the list. But I know, at seventeen, that I won't meet a Mormon husband at UCLA. Cole is leaving for mission soon. I'm really sad to see him go, but I know how young I am and that there are other exciting experiences ahead of me. I don't plan on waiting for him, and while he's gone, dating other Mormon guys is important to me.

Still, I go back and forth between BYU and UCLA. I save all the UCLA recruitment letters that arrive at my house. I fantasize about wearing blue and gold.

But eventually, Lauren commits to BYU for me, so other coaches can see in the online portal that I'm going to BYU. When I find out, I say, "Lauren, when did I verbally commit to you?" But it's funny.

A FEW DAYS BEFORE Cole leaves for mission, he tells me he's worried about me. We're at the beach together, and we walk to this lookout area, where he turns to me in his swim trunks and tank top. He's gotten skinny since he went vegan, and there's a look in his eyes I've never seen before. He says, "Boys in college will use you. You have to be careful."

I tell him he's being crazy. I'm going to BYU, where my sister lives. I'll be playing three hours of tennis a day. "I literally don't know what you're talking about."

But he's so serious. "Don't drink," he says. "Don't date bad boys."

"Cole," I tell him, "I'm going to be fine."

But he warns me again to be good. He seems uneasy. There's a breeze, and he's staring at me. It feels like a premonition.

FOUR

Coto de Caza is a wealthy area, but growing up, I don't understand that my family is rich. We don't buy Charmin toilet paper. My mom and I hide our manicures from my dad. In our house, leaving the lights on is a high crime. And running the air-conditioning—even in the summer, when it's a hundred degrees outside—is akin to first-degree murder. When I learn to drive, I inherit a 1995 Lexus SC. It's white with a tan interior. My dad calls it the White Stallion. I call it the White Turd because there are so many things wrong with it. The seats are cracked. There's foam coming out of the leather. And if you turn off the AC, the whole car shuts off, even if you're driving on the freeway.

My dad's rule is that if any of his kids get a full-ride scholarship to college, they get a new car. I don't know when mine is coming, but I'm excited when BYU pays for me to fly out to Provo for the weekend. I've already committed to play there, but I get to do a recruitment trip anyway. For fun, mostly. And for an excuse to spend time with Lauren and the team.

I've never traveled alone before. I feel anxious on the plane, but better when I see Lauren. She knows all of my secrets: like how I goofed off with all of my other tennis coaches, which is why my mom fired them and started coaching me herself. She knows that once, when my mom was feeding me balls at a court near our house, she said, "Don't hit like this, hit like *this*," and stepped forward to show me her footwork then fell, ripping her pants. She knows that I laughed so hard at my mom tripping on a perfectly flat court that I had to run laps. And she knows that, to my family, I'm uncoachable, even though tennis has always come naturally to me.

Lauren acts like my coach and my sister, setting me up in her spare room with clean sheets and towels, then reminding me of our meeting with the BYU athletic director the next morning. I can tell she takes her job seriously. She's relatively new to the role as head coach. And she's in the tough position of rebuilding a program that fell apart after the last head coach, who only lasted a year, caused lots of the top players, including McCall, to transfer.

We sit on the bed, and Lauren tells me it's a program in transition. What she means is that it's a program where freshmen like me will have the opportunity to play number one and number two. I like that. I want to be the best.

In college tennis, coaches pick six girls to play per match: a number one, a number two, a number three, and so on. As number one, it's your responsibility to lead the team. Each team's number one player competes against their opponent's top player. It's a lot of pressure. But I know I'm good enough to get the spot. I'm BYU's first blue-chip recruit since McCall.

LAUREN TAKES ME ON a golf-cart tour of campus, showing off the indoor and outdoor courts, the weight room, and taking me to a meeting with the athletic director, Tom Holmoe, in his office in the Student Athlete Building.

I like Tom right away. He's tall: a former football player who was a defensive back at BYU before playing for the 49ers and coaching at Cal Berkeley. Tom oversees twenty-two sports at BYU, but he takes his time talking to me. He makes me feel special.

BECAUSE IT'S HALLOWEEN, THERE are parties that weekend. Lauren encourages me to go out with the team. I wear one of McCall's old costumes. It's a cop outfit made out of fake leather.

One of the girls on the team, Meghan, is from Southern California. She and I know each other from the tennis circuit. It's nice to have a built-in friend, especially because it's clear that I'm out of my element.

On the drive to the party, people are already drinking. This isn't my first exposure to alcohol, but it's the first time I realize people at BYU actually party. I think this is crazy. BYU's honor code means that you can get kicked out of school for drinking or having sex outside of marriage, and students can report one another online. I didn't realize anyone would be willing to risk that. Apparently, I was wrong.

I don't drink that night, but I clock who does. And I'm almost positive that Lauren, who never stepped out of line in college, has no idea what's happening.

The Halloween party is in a warehouse. It almost looks like a sports facility: there's turf on the floor and two levels. I'm still innocent, still seventeen, but single. I get dirty on the dance floor. Next year, when I go back to the same party, my abuser will freak out anytime a guy gets near me. But for now, I'm free.

I dance with Meghan, a guy from BYU volleyball, and at one point, a creepy older guy who comes up behind me and grabs my hips.

I shimmy away to avoid him. He gives me bad vibes.

Our team has VIP passes, meaning we can go to the upstairs section of the club. Meghan and I decide to take the elevator up to get a break from the chaos, but when I walk inside, Meghan's not with me. I turn and see the man who tried to grind on me following me in with two of his friends. Meghan's still on the dance floor, tipsily saying hi to someone she ran into. I feel frozen. I do nothing as the man pushes me against the wall of the elevator, smacking my head into the metal. He starts tugging up my dress. I know I should run away or scream, but I can't. The doors are closing. Suddenly Meghan pushes inside, yells, "Don't touch her!" and pulls me back onto the dance floor. I don't tell anyone but her what happened. But I keep reliving the moment I turned and saw the man getting in the elevator after me. I don't know what would've happened if Meghan hadn't pulled me out, but I wonder why I couldn't move.

I try not to think about it. I dance with Meghan, and other tennis girls, and that volleyball player from the men's team who will go on to play in the Olympics. I can't believe the moment in the elevator actually happened.

I'm rattled, but I do my best to shake it off. It doesn't even occur to me to report it. There's no one to even report it to. And I know it won't impact the trajectory of my life. I'm still going to BYU for tennis. Lauren will still be my coach. The only thing that's different is that now I know people party at BYU.

BACK IN CALIFORNIA, I win two tennis tournaments. After one, when I beat a girl named Alyssa who'd been demolishing me since we were ten, I get invited to a clinic at Woodbridge Tennis Academy in Irvine with some of the top high school players in the United States.

Everyone involved is going on scholarship to a top-20 program. The competition is fierce. I finally feel like I'm pushing myself, and I fall in love with the sport in a new way. For the first time, I want to win for myself instead of my mom. And I like the players I meet, especially Alyssa.

The Woodbridge clinic is twice a week. The drills are intense. We stand at the net and hit volleys at each other as hard as we can. We sprint. We do point play. I thrive on the competition. I don't mind that the drive to Irvine takes half an hour, or that I'm exhausted when I come home. I have a whole new friend group.

Plus, since I'm getting better at tennis, I'm winning more, which makes me and my parents happy. It also means they have to follow through on their promise to get me a car.

I test-drive an Audi and fall in love, but I know there's no way my dad's going to buy me something so expensive. And I'm totally happy with a used car. But just in case he decides to spoil me, I let him know my favorite is the latest edition white A4 with a gray interior.

On Christmas, we open presents in the living room by the tree. Everyone's wearing their matching Christmas pajamas. We're just starting on the pile when my brother Alex hands me a package. My dad stands and says, "Don't open that yet, Mayci." I have a feeling it's a car key. My dad is a man of his word. Everyone goes back and forth about the present for a second, and then my dad says, "Fine. Go for it."

I pull off the wrapping and find a car key. I get up and walk outside with everyone following me. There's an older-model Audi A4 in the driveway. It's charcoal colored. I'm stoked. I've wanted a car—this car—for months. And here it is.

But when I get inside, the windshield is cracked, there's dirt by the pedals and dust caked on the dashboard. It smells slightly stale, like old fast food. I'm still happy, but I'm also confused. My dad is meticulous. I know that if he bought me a car, new or used, it would be perfect. He wouldn't give me one with a windshield crack.

I look out the car window and see my mom laughing. Now I'm annoyed. I can't tell if she's laughing at me or at my car, but I thank my parents and go back inside so we can finish opening presents. The floor is covered in wrapping paper and ribbons. Usually, we clean up, but instead my dad says, "Should we go drive your car around?"

I say yes. Absolutely. We go back outside, but the car isn't in the driveway anymore. I look around, clutching the key. The car isn't on the street either.

My mom is laughing again. She opens the garage. The door lifts to reveal my brother sitting behind the steering wheel of a brand-new white A4 with a gray interior. My dream car. The other one belonged to my dad's friend. My parents had borrowed it to prank me.

FIVE

IT'S NEW YEAR'S AND I'M AT A MORMON DANCE AGAIN. I'M there, like everyone else, to be set up. My friend Sam wants me to meet a guy whose name I won't use, but who my parents call the asshole, I call my abuser, and we'll call Dick. I've seen pictures of Dick and think he's cute. I'm intrigued by the setup. And I'm excited that, at seventeen, I've gotten into the church's Young Single Adult dance at the Dave & Buster's in Irvine, which is supposed to be for single Mormons between eighteen and thirty years old.

The first thing I notice about Dick is that he's as handsome in real life as he is in photos. He's tall—five-eleven—sculpted, and clean-cut. His hair is perfect. He has a six-pack. Everything about him is attractive except his voice. It's not high-pitched exactly, but it's weird. I'm totally caught off guard by it. It gives me the ick.

I try to ignore it, but it distracts me.

Still, the vibes are there. I'm pretty sure we're going to kiss at midnight. I've only ever kissed Mark, Cole, and two other guys: one right after Cole left for his mission and I felt like I had to move on, and another over the summer in Utah. And I've never made out with someone the first day we've met.

The idea of kissing Dick at the dance feels exciting and grown-up. And I want to do something wild. I want to step out of my comfort zone.

During the countdown to midnight, everyone pairs off. I step closer to

Dick. He's so tall. I tilt my chin up. When it's midnight, we lean in. The kiss is surprisingly good. I feel giddy.

Looking back, the setup feels forced: Dick is who I'm supposed to want, so I convince myself that I want him. He comes from a good family. He's Mormon. And Sam has made a point to tell me that Dick is rich.

I like that he used to be a bad boy, too, even though I don't know exactly what that means. Maybe he used to drink. Maybe he even smoked.

DICK LIVES FORTY MINUTES from my parents in Anaheim. I go over there the next night with Sam and some of our other friends.

When I park, the first thing I think is maybe Sam and I have a different definition of rich. Dick's house is nice. But it's nothing spectacular.

The next day, Dick drives to see me in Coto, and we hang out at my parents' house in the bonus room. Two days later, it's my mom's birthday. I invite Dick to come out to dinner to celebrate with our family. My brother Alex is dating someone, too, but she can't make it. When Alex mentions her name at the restaurant, Dick starts laughing. We all look at him across the table, and he admits that he made out with Alex's girlfriend a year earlier. My family thinks it's funny. I do too. My parents aren't obsessed with Dick, but they're happy for him to spend time with us. They don't see any red flags. And neither do I.

Our family has a tradition of doing different day trips over the holidays. One day, we drive to San Diego to get tacos, then go to a Yorkie breeder so my parents can get a puppy. We sit next to each other in the car on the drive back to Coto, holding hands on the seat. Dick and I never say we're a couple, but we've become one right away. I see him every day between New Year's and when he goes back to BYU.

AFTER DICK LEAVES FOR college, we talk constantly. I never worry that he's going to hook up with someone else. He's anxious I'm going to, though.

He texts and calls me all the time. I don't see this behavior as problematic. Dick is cute and tall. He goes to BYU. He plays club ice hockey. He sends me flowers, and when they arrive my mom and I both think he's Prince Charming.

But Dick and I fight a lot. Or at least, he fights a lot. He gets mad at me for things that seem totally normal.

One day, when I'm driving with Alyssa and some of the guys from the Woodbridge clinic, he calls me. He knows we all get dinner once a week after playing. There are two guys and three girls in our group. We're all friends—there's nothing romantic between any of us. But Dick is still jealous. When I answer the phone in the car, he says something snarky about one of the guys. It's rude, and I hang up on him, embarrassed.

Alyssa asks why I'm dating him. One of the other guys does too. They both say he's possessive. I don't want to admit it, even to myself, but I know they have a point. Dick is way more insecure than I originally thought. He's sadder than I originally thought too. He constantly needs validation. It's exhausting.

One day, when my friends from the clinic are hanging out at my parents' house, he freaks out because I'm spending time with other guys. Another time, when he's home from school, he says he thinks he can beat me at tennis, so my mom takes the two of us to the court to teach him how to play. She feeds him balls. When he misses a few, he gets mad and hits them off the court. I pretend it's funny so my mom doesn't worry, but it's a turn-off. This man is not a pro tennis player—he's hardly even held a racket before—so I'm not entirely sure why he thinks he should be playing like one. By the time we're done, there are balls all over the tennis club roof.

I GO VISIT DICK in Utah. He lives off-campus in housing called Alpine Village. It's only a block from BYU, and it feels a little like a dorm. There's a pool, dirty carpet, and chipped paint on the walls. The room itself is tiny: space for a closet, a small desk, and a twin bed. But to me, it's the coolest place

I've ever been. It's living alone! I don't stay with Dick—we haven't done more than make out, and my family would never allow it—but it's fun to see. I can imagine spending time there when I come to BYU in the fall.

In bed at Lauren's town house that night, I feel ready to be in college: ready to stay out as late as I want; ready to sleep over at Dick's. I tell myself he'll be less controlling when we live in the same state. He'll chill out.

The next day is Valentine's Day. Dick and I go on a date to the Cheesecake Factory. I wear a black peplum top, jeans, and red stripper heels I can barely walk in.

He gives me a Tiffany necklace with two little hearts—one turquoise and one silver—and later, when we're parked in the car outside Lauren's house, he tells me he loves me by writing it with his finger in the fog of his windshield and then tracing a heart around the letters. I say it back even though I'm not sure I feel it. It seems like the thing a girlfriend is supposed to do. And I don't know what love is. I like the way it feels when Dick winds his arms around my shoulders. I like feeling special. Chosen.

THE THING WITH DICK is that things are never good for long.

When he says he can't fly back to California for my winter formal, he gets furious that I want to bring a guy friend as my date. I push back, and we break up. But a few days later, he love-bombs me, I swoon, and we get back together. This becomes our pattern. He does something crazy, I break up with him, he says and does nice things, we get back together. Again and again and again.

On one of his trips to California, Dick is supposed to pick me up so we can go to L.A. to visit McCall, but I have this sick feeling. It's almost like I have the flu. Our church is doing a road show: basically a play where the youth all have parts. After going to a rehearsal, I lay on the carpeted floor of my parents' bedroom and tell my mom I don't want to go.

"What do you mean?" she asks.

Dick is downstairs. It's embarrassing to send him away, but I have this premonition.

TOLD YOU SO

"Why don't you at least go to lunch with him?" my mom suggests. "You can always come back after. You don't have to go all the way up to UCLA."

But I don't want to go anywhere with Dick. My body is telling me there's something off. It's giving me a warning sign. I don't listen. Instead, I stand up, drag my feet across my parents' carpeted room, and go downstairs, where Dick is waiting for me.

SIX

"JUST SEND ME ONE PICTURE."

I read the text again. I don't want to send Dick nudes. I've never done anything like that in my life. But he's been asking a lot. He sends another text. "Come on, Mayci." I get out of bed and make sure the door to my room is closed.

I feel embarrassed taking off my clothes. But I take two pictures on Snapchat to get Dick to stop asking. I don't know if he can save them or share them. I hope he can't.

I assume sending him pictures will get him off my back. Instead, the pressure increases. After I send those first pictures, he wants more. It's never enough.

When he comes back to town, he wants to go past making out. I'm not ready. I've told him that repeatedly. But one afternoon, when we're kissing in the bonus room at my parents' house, he puts his hand down my pants. There's literally no consent. One second we're kissing, and the next, his clammy hand is on my vagina. I don't stop him. I'm not happy it's happening, but I can't say I'm actively upset either. I sort of disassociate. And then it's over. I'm zero percent turned on the entire time.

What's weird is that after it happens, I start to think it's kind of OK. It's like that with every step. I never want to send nudes. I never want Dick to finger me. But after I do it, it breaks the seal. It becomes free game.

That night, we're supposed to have dinner at his parents' house. I don't love going over there and spending time with his family. At the beginning of our relationship, I took everything Dick said about them at face value—that he was the victim, that his brother was mean, that he always demeaned him—but one afternoon when I was at their house, Dick's brother made one small, teasing comment, and Dick freaked out and started screaming. Their mom came in and started yelling at everyone. It was so awkward that I walked out of the room. Dick's brother didn't even do anything, and Dick was calling him an asshole and completely losing his mind.

I don't want to relive that. And I'm not trying to get fingered again.

THE WHOLE DRIVE TO Anaheim, Dick tells me that nobody's going to be home before the dinner. He sounds excited, but I'm scared.

The second we get to his house, Dick leads me to his room, where we start making out on the bed. I can tell he expects me to give him a hand job because he touched me earlier. I'm so afraid of his penis—I don't want to look at it, let alone touch it. I don't want to look him in the eye, either, so I alternate staring at the ceiling and at his bedspread. I feel grossed-out and complicit and guilty. I'm trying to give him a hand job—probably badly, because I have no idea what I'm doing and we don't have any lube—when I hear the back door open. I'm in my underwear. Dick has his shirt and pants off. I jump off the bed and lunge for my clothes. I'm already afraid of his mom after the yelling incident, and the back door is close to Dick's bedroom.

Dick is panicking too. He grabs his pants, and as he pulls them up, his belt buckle jingles incredibly loudly. I know his mom can hear it. She walks in just as he's gotten his pants on. She looks at me—my face flushed, my clothes wrinkled—and at Dick, who's panting, and says, "You know you're not supposed to have girls in your room."

He says, "OK."

There's an awkward beat, and then she leaves the door open and goes back into the hall. I feel terrible. I don't want to stay for family dinner, but I have no idea how to leave. His mom is making Cafe Rio–style sweet pork for their extended family. She's been working on it all day.

A little later, Dick and I go into the dining room. There are a ton of people there: friends, extended family, siblings. I stand beside Dick, nervous to meet everyone.

Before we get food, his mom looks at me and says, "Mayci, can you give the opening prayer?" I know she knows Dick and I were fooling around and that this is her way of telling me. I hardly know his family. Her husband or son should give the opening prayer, not a guest. It catches me off guard. I stumble through the whole prayer, mortified. It's so embarrassing.

SEVEN

I MEET WITH MY BISHOP IN HIS OFFICE. HE'S IN HIS MID-fifties. Tall. His dark hair graying at his temples. He sits behind a large wooden desk. I take the chair opposite him, leaving the ones on the sides of the room empty. I start to cry the second I sit down. I'm not a crier. But I feel humiliated telling this middle-aged man, "My boyfriend touched me and I touched him." Repenting like this is normal for Mormons. It's part of belonging to the church. But it's uncomfortable for me, at seventeen, to sit alone with an older man and talk about fingering and hand jobs. When I think about my kids doing this, my skin crawls.

The bishop says he's glad I'm crying. "I see remorse," he tells me, clasping his hands on the desk. "That's good. You feel guilty for this sin."

I leave his office feeling slightly better, but a couple weeks later, Dick and I are messing around again. Dick tells me it's fine. Normal, even. It's what good girlfriends in serious relationships do. But I feel terrible. I didn't even last a few weeks.

I GET A TEXT from an unknown number: "Hey, this is Dick's friend. Dick is in the hospital right now. I'll call you when I have news."

I have to read the message twice. I'm in Palm Springs for the Easter Bowl with Alyssa. It's an hour before our doubles match. I need to focus, but I can't tell if the text is a joke. Dick is at school in Utah and I'm in California. He knows how important this tournament is. I respond asking if he's joking, and the unknown number sends a photo of a hospital bed. I know enough to check if it's fake. But it's not a random Google image. It looks real.

I panic. I think something is horribly wrong. I imagine Dick in surgery, Dick bleeding, Dick hurt. I've always been squeamish—I hate giving blood—and the idea of him hooked up to an IV makes me nauseous.

I'm supposed to be warming up and focusing. This is a major national tournament, and I don't want to let Alyssa down. But I can't stop thinking about Dick. I text him and the unknown number for updates, sure this is a life-or-death thing. No response.

During the game, I can't focus. Alyssa is playing well. I can tell she wants the win. But my serve is off. I'm missing crosscourt shots that should be easy winners. We lose the match and the tournament.

Afterward, Dick tells me it was all a joke. He was visiting a friend in the hospital and wanted to play a prank on me. Alyssa's mom thinks that's horrible. She tells me to break up with him. My mom thinks it's weird too. "Dick is clearly an attention-seeker," she says. I know what he did was wrong. I know he sabotaged me.

I break up with him again. I say it's unfair he played mind games with me. I tell him how messed up it is that he ruined the tournament for me. He sends me flowers and begs me to take him back. I relent. We get back together a few days later.

IT'S MAY AND DICK'S home for the summer. He's working for his dad's business. I'm playing tennis and finishing high school. Dick invites me to spend the weekend with his family at their house in Lake Havasu, Arizona. My parents are OK with it as long as I don't leave tennis practice early to get there. I'm nervous, though. Dick's parents will be there, but I know he wants more to happen between us anyway.

Dick picks me up from tennis and we drive the four hours to Lake Havasu. It's fun to be in the car together for so long. We laugh and tell stories.

TOLD YOU SO

The lake house isn't anything special. It's clear Dick's family spends their money on toys and not interiors. There's a speedboat, Jet Skis, a second boat, and a prop plane that I swear I won't get in. Dick's family obviously doesn't want us sleeping in the same room, so I get the guest room. I'm relieved to have some space to myself.

When I wake up the first morning, I stay in the room for a long time savoring the solitude. I don't know if Dick's up yet, and I'm still a little afraid of his mom. She has a strong personality.

That day, we go boating. I've never wakeboarded before, and I love it. My mom never let me do anything that could injure me or hurt my tennis career, and it's way harder than I expect. Dick is amazing at it. I feel attracted to him as I watch him glide effortlessly over the water.

DICK'S AUNT AND UNCLE arrive that night, meaning I have to give up the guest room. His mom moves me to the bonus room, which is where Dick, his brother, and his brother's girlfriend have all been sleeping. There's a TV in there, along with a bunch of couches. I preferred having a room to myself. It afforded me a barrier from the constant pressure to make out. When I'm around Dick, my chin hurts from his scruff rubbing against it.

Once everyone else falls asleep, Dick leads me out into the living room. We start kissing on the couch and things escalate until suddenly he's asking for a hand job. I've been trying to stay away from sexual sins ever since I repented because I don't want to have to talk to the bishop again, but Dick pushes me to touch his penis, and I do.

When he finishes, I freak out. I've never seen cum before, and I definitely didn't expect it to go shooting into the air. I don't know what to do. It smells gross, and it's so messy. I'm saying, "Oh my gosh, oh my gosh, what is this?" And he's shushing me because everyone's sleeping and he doesn't want me to wake them up.

The next night, the same thing happens, except instead of the living room, he leads me over to the side of the house. We make out on the rocks by the trash cans. I feel guilty and worried we're going to get caught. I give him another hand job, even though I don't want to. This time, he cums onto the rocks.

I HAVE MY FIRST drink on this trip. I've barely been around alcohol before. But Dick's aunt and uncle aren't Mormon. His aunt left the church and his uncle was never part of it. They make piña coladas and offer to let me and Dick try some.

I'm scared, but Dick pulls me aside and says that in the eyes of the church, doing sexual things is way worse than drinking alcohol. I look up at him. I know he has a past. He's mentioned that his parents made him do therapy; that he's been prescribed meds for anxiety and depression but that he doesn't take them. He's told me he's tried alcohol, too, but said he doesn't drink anymore. I wonder, as he leads me back toward his aunt and uncle, if that was a lie. Maybe he's never stopped. But how bad is that?

The piña colada is good. I can't even taste any alcohol.

LATER THAT NIGHT, DICK and I break into the freezer, where his aunt and uncle are storing the Grey Goose. I'm curious to see what it tastes like when it's not mixed into a fruity drink. Standing barefoot in the dark kitchen, I sip from the bottle and gag. It's disgusting, but I get a very slight buzz, which I like. We go into the living room, where we play Jenga with his aunt and uncle, who are tipsy too. It's fun to play and share the secret. Dick's brother, who's on a good path, doesn't have any.

THE LAST NIGHT OF the trip, we all go outside and watch Dick's brother propose to his girlfriend. He floats the ring down the river to her. It's really special. Everyone is moved except Dick, who laughs obnoxiously. His behavior bugs me. I don't understand why he can't just be happy for his brother. I wonder if he's secretly been taking more swigs from the bottle of Grey Goose.

I elbow him and say, "Can you stop laughing?"

He looks at me and laughs harder. My prom is coming up, and Dick starts joking about asking me to go to prom by floating something down the river too. It's not funny. But his whole family joins in. They keep saying, "Are you gonna do that for Mayci?"

All my high school friends are getting asked to prom in nice ways. I want that too—just like every girl does. And I hate that Dick's family is mocking it. It makes me feel like a little girl.

THINGS ARE BETTER ON the drive home from Arizona. Being with Dick is fun again. We're in his souped-up Mustang. It looks hideous, but it's fast and loud. We're laughing as we rev the engine and roar past other cars. I mention that my friend has invited me to a big concert. She has backstage passes.

He asks, "Who are you gonna go with?"

"Well, my friend," I say, "she got the tickets."

"Are other guys gonna be there?"

I'm supposed to go with a big group. I'm so excited: the radio station that's promoting it, 105.9, is one of my favorites. It's what I listen to when I'm driving to and from Woodbridge.

"Probably," I say. "It's my friend's friends."

Dick takes his eyes off the road and says, "What makes you think you're going to go to that?" We're going 100 miles an hour.

I tell him to slow down. He doesn't. I ask again. He keeps speeding, but now he's yelling too. He says I can't go to the concert if there are going to be other men there. He says I can't go to *anything* if there are going to be other men there.

We get in a huge fight. He's going too fast, swerving all over the road.

I wish I could say that I go to the concert. But I don't.

EIGHT

IT'S PROM NIGHT AND DICK WANTS TO HAVE SEX. WE'RE watching a movie in the living room at my parents' house with my friends Emily and Sam. It's late. My hair is down and stringy. My makeup feels crusty from sweating on the dance floor. I can't believe Dick wants to talk about sex now.

I turn to him on the beanbag chair where we're cuddling and say, "I'm not having sex tonight. I'm saving myself for marriage and you know that."

"Prom night is supposed to be a huge night in someone's life."

"OK," I say.

"We love each other."

"OK," I say again. I'm nodding as Dick talks, but in my head, I'm like, *What in the world is this guy thinking? Number one, we're at my parents' house with my friends. Where is he even thinking this is going to happen? Number two, I'm Mormon. I'm not having sex outside of marriage, which I've communicated repeatedly. And I'm definitely not doing it on a beanbag in the living room while two other people watch a movie.*

Dick starts kissing me. To end the fight, I kiss him back. He fingers me. I don't want it, but I don't stop him. I'd rather let him finger me—even though I'm dry as the Mojave Desert—than argue. The fight just isn't worth it.

A FEW DAYS LATER, Dick and I are at the movies. We're seeing *Edge of Tomorrow*. I want to pay attention to the plot, but the whole time, Dick has his hands down my pants. I'm not even remotely wet. Nothing about getting fingered under a blanket at a crowded movie theater is enjoyable for me. I can feel Dick's fingernail digging into my skin and it's starting to piss me off. I try to pluck his hands out of my pants, but he keeps going back in. I'm like, *What are you getting out of this? Who is this fun for? Definitely not me.*

Later, I text Dick about how guilty I feel for continuing to mess around. Ever since Arizona, things have escalated. It's the opposite of what I wanted. We haven't had sex, but we've done other things, and I feel ashamed.

One day, my sister McCall reads one of our texts and tells my dad that she thinks we've messed up. He doesn't bring it up with me until church on Sunday, when he pulls me aside after the first hour and asks to talk.

He and I end up skipping the second hour and sitting in the car. He tells me that he knows that Dick and I are fooling around. He says he understands that we're teenagers and that our hormones are crazy, but he's clear that I need to fix the issue. He tries to help me. He's not mad. He doesn't even tell my mom, who would be furious. He just wants to make sure I'm being safe and I'm not going to screw up even more.

I'm embarrassed to have this conversation, but more than that, I'm grateful that my mom doesn't know. The women in church are held to a higher standard, and I know she wouldn't understand. She would tell me that men can't control themselves, but that women can because we're wired differently. She'd get emotional about it too. My dad is more open-minded. He gets it. Even though I'm terrified and humiliated that he knows, I appreciate that he's approached me quietly to try to fix it together. He tells me he wants me to talk to the bishop. I agree.

Again, I sit in the chair in the center of the room. Again, the bishop takes his seat behind his desk. Again, I say I messed up. But this time, the conversation goes badly. The bishop is stern and disappointed. He tells me I can't keep doing this. Everyone who goes to BYU needs a recommendation from a religious leader. If you're Mormon, you meet with your bishop. If you're not Mormon, you still have to follow the honor code—no lying, drinking, sex before marriage, and so on—but you also need an endorsement from your religious leader or a bishop. The ecclesiastical endorsement is part of your application. You can't go to BYU without it.

The bishop threatens to take my ecclesiastical endorsement away. He says to keep it I need to see him more frequently and read a 1969 book called *The Miracle of Forgiveness* that basically says that sexual sin is right below murder.

Reading it, I feel completely horrible, like I'm the worst person in the world. But I'm relieved to have a plan to get my endorsement back. I'm relieved to have a plan to get to BYU.

NINE

TENNIS IS A WINTER SPORT, WHICH MEANS I DON'T HAVE to be at school until Labor Day.

At the end of August, my parents and I drive out to Utah. In the car, my dad tells me I need to break up with Dick. He says, "You're going to have a blast in college. It's time to meet a lot of new people, to gain a lot of friends and have new experiences. You won't have that if you stay with Dick. He's going to smother you. He'll try to control you." I nod but don't say anything. "How about this?" he asks, looking over at me. "Pray on it."

I tell him I will, and then my mom changes the subject.

When we get to campus, my mom sets up my room with teal sheets and a zebra-striped comforter. I live in the old dorms, because Lauren wants me to be close to the tennis courts. I can walk to them in under ten minutes.

BYU is a culture shock for many reasons. Everyone is weirdly wholesome, almost childlike. People walk around singing Disney and church songs. At preseason tennis practice, I'm not allowed to wear tank tops. And no one on our team can wear spandex in the weight room because it could be distracting for the guys. I've grown up competing in spaghetti straps and mini tennis skirts. The first time I try on my BYU-issued tennis skirt, it drives me crazy. I'm like, *How am I supposed to play wearing this?* I decide the best option is to roll it up.

My roommate is nice but a little odd. She decorates her bed with thirty stuffed animals. I like stuffed animals enough, but thirty feels excessive, and when we go to church together, she turns to me and whispers, "Mayci." I face her. "Look," she says. I glance down. She's petting one of her stuffed animals. I have no idea what to say, so I mumble, "Oh, cool," and go back to listening to whatever the members are talking about.

That's the last time my roommate and I hang out outside of living together. I spend most of my time with Dick. At first, I make an effort not to party. I don't want to get in trouble with the honor code. I want to avoid temptation. And I don't want to be associated with bad influences.

But Dick lives with hockey guys who are constantly drinking and smoking weed. I make it a week before he badgers me into sleeping over there. Soon after that, Dick gets antsy and starts pressuring me to give him blow jobs. I don't enjoy giving them. It hurts my neck and jaw. And I never like when he eats me out. I spend most of the time he's down there wanting to kick him in the head with my foot. I used to like hooking up with him. But now pretending to orgasm feels like a chore. And I really don't like that he's pressuring me to have sex.

DICK WANTS TO BE with me all the time. The second I finish practice he expects me to come back to his apartment and not leave. I don't want my life to be that small. I want to hang out with friends and meet people and see my baby niece Presley, who Lauren's given birth to over the summer. But Dick is insistent. I have recurring nightmares where I'm stuck in a room and people—not just Dick—are drugging me and using me for sex. Each time I wake up, I'm scared and sweating.

Dick starts picking me up at practice so I can't hang out with anyone else. He says it's a nice favor because parking is hard to find at BYU. But I'd rather walk back to my dorm alone and in peace.

Lauren notices. She tells my parents how controlling Dick is. When they ask me if everything's OK, I blow them off. I want the college experience. And part of me believes I love Dick. I've already sinned so much with him. It feels like I'm in too deep to back out. Who else would even want me?

When Dick tells me, again, that drinking and smoking weed aren't nearly as bad in the church's eyes as sex, I listen to him. A lot of BYU athletes drink. As long as I don't get caught, it doesn't seem like it's hurting anyone. Plus, I'm tired of fighting about it.

Soon after, Dick says I should try smoking weed. I'm at his apartment with Sam, who set us up, and his girlfriend. They tell me I should try using the G Pen. They say it's for weed, but I later learn it's for wax: something even more potent and synthetic.

I've never done anything like this before. But Sam and Dick promise it'll leave my system faster than smoking regular weed. I don't know when drug testing will show up at practice next, so I'm anxious. But I trust Dick and Sam. I take a hit of the pen, breathing in and out. I don't feel anything. They all tell me I'm not inhaling right. They're high already, laughing and goofy. I don't get it. Am I doing something wrong? They say I really need to hold the weed in my lungs. I take a huge hit and hold it in until I have a coughing fit. Tears stream down my face. I can't catch my breath. I run to the bathroom and cough into the sink, almost puking. When I finally catch my breath and come back into the living room, everyone is laughing at me.

Dick says, "Oh shit, you're going to get so high."

I do. I lie in Dick's single bed, my face burning, and look at the zebra painting he's stuck to the wall. I'm convinced the zebra is talking to me. But I'm also convinced I'm in a dream. I keep thinking I've woken up, but the dream continues. I feel scared and start crying. I don't want anyone to see that I'm upset. I cover my face with my hands, sure I'll never feel normal again.

THE NEXT MORNING, I decide that getting high was interesting. I even think I might try it again sometime, until Dick tells me the drug doesn't stay in your system for a couple days. It can last weeks. I panic and drive myself to a smoke shop in Provo, where I buy a drink that's supposed to mask the

THC in your system. I take off the label and keep it in my tennis bag. I tell myself that if drug testing shows up at practice, I'll chug it really fast and pray it works. In the meantime, I drink water and cranberry juice like it's my job.

In the end, drug testing doesn't happen at practice, which is incredibly lucky, because I later learn that if you test positive for any of the ingredients in the THC-masking drink, you fail the test anyway since BYU assumes you're hiding something.

TEN

DICK WANTS ME TO DRINK EVERY NIGHT. I ENJOY IT NOW. Or at least, I enjoy it more than I did in Arizona. But it's still stressful to go out at BYU. There's the worry that someone's going to report you for violating the honor code. And Dick freaks out when other guys look at me. He's always trying to start fights.

Some nights, we have fun together. But most of the time, he leans into his victim mentality and blames me for how depressed or anxious he feels. I see so many red flags with him, but I'm not equipped to deal with them. My sisters have never messed up; they've never stepped out of line. And even though my brother doesn't follow all the church's guidelines, there's a double standard there. He's a guy and he's not on scholarship. I'm worried that if I tell anyone that I'm starting to feel uncomfortable with Dick—and why—I'll get in trouble for breaking the honor code. I'm trapped.

I'm too young to understand I need to leave Dick, and as things get worse between us, it becomes harder to. Dick starts taking pictures of me drinking. He doesn't say they're blackmail, and at first, I don't think of them that way. But I know if he ever submits them to BYU, I'll be kicked out in an instant. I try not to think about what that would mean for me and my family. My parents would be humiliated. And it would be terrible for Lauren. It would mess everything up.

IN OCTOBER, DICK'S PARENTS ask him to move out of the hockey house. They think the team is a bad influence. Dick's new apartment is a couple buildings away in the same complex. Instead of his zebra painting, he sticks a black tree decal to the wall above his bed. I start to think of this new apartment as a sex dungeon. Dick and I haven't slept together yet, but we've done everything else, and whenever I'm over at his place, Dick expects us to mess around constantly. Nothing about this is fun anymore, especially because he's so angry all the time. He always picks a fight, even when there's nothing to fight about. Maybe I took too long to respond to a text. Maybe I wanted to go to Swig, aka my favorite soda shop, with a girlfriend. He's having stomach pain, paranoia, and anxiety. And his anger issues are getting worse.

Sometimes when we're hanging out he suddenly turns into a totally different person. I never know what his triggers are, although drinking makes it much worse. I'll look at his face and not even recognize him. His eyes go black. When that happens, I know I need to shut my mouth and be a good girl. Or else.

BYU ICE HOCKEY IS a club sport as opposed to Division 1, so Dick can't access the Student Athlete Building. It becomes a safe place for me to get away from him. There are tutors and places for athletes to socialize. It pisses him off that he can't get inside, but I'm grateful.

One night, when he's tipsy, he gets paranoid that I go to the Student Athlete Building to talk to other guys. I tell him it's fine, don't worry, relax, and he grabs me by the neck, chokes me, then throws me onto his bed.

Another night, in another jealous fit, he tries to cut his wrists in front of me. I want to stop him. When I reach for the razor blade, he slices my thigh. He says it's an accident, but a drip of blood runs from my thigh to my knee. I hate blood. I've never been able to handle it. Dick knows that. I believe he's doing this on purpose.

I realize, cleaning my leg in his bathroom, that something is really wrong here—that my dad was right. Dick is trying to control me. Part of me feels that I'm being abused, too, but I don't want to admit it. It's too painful and embarrassing. I don't want to be a victim. Plus, since I can't get help, it's better to just be in denial and deal with it.

I take pictures of my leg anyway. I don't know what I'll do with the photos. I can't show my parents—they'll just bring me home. And Lauren can't do anything. She's stuck between me and BYU. But I want to have proof for myself.

When I wake up at Dick's apartment the next morning, I discover all the pictures have been deleted from my phone.

I go to tennis practice and play badly. When Lauren tries to coach me, I have an attitude on the court. Later, I get a message from my mom. She says Lauren told her I didn't play well. I read the message in Dick's apartment, then look over at him and think, *Seriously? How is this my life? If they only knew what I was really dealing with.*

TENNIS IS AN ANCHOR and an escape, but the time commitment is intense. And I'm not enjoying it as much as I used to. Back home, I played in clinic with guys who were going on a full ride to UCLA—the best of the best. The level of competition at BYU isn't as high. The players are good, but the games are slower-paced. And I've been playing for so long that the routine of lifting and practice starts to feel mundane.

We're in preseason, so we're doing a lot of workouts. Our trainers want to know how fast we can run two miles. How long does it take us to sprint a lap around the track? Can we hold a four-minute plank? How much can we leg press?

The worst day is the beep test. It's a drill where we have to sprint between two cones at increasingly fast intervals. The whole team is competitive about it, so naturally we're all anxious leading up to it. I want to prove myself. I haven't officially earned the number one spot yet, but I want to show that I'm ready for it. I push myself so hard I come down with the flu the next day. But it's worth it. I finish with the fastest time.

ELEVEN

DICK AND I ARE STILL BREAKING UP AND GETTING BACK together. When I work on a biology project with a guy who adds me on Facebook, Dick loses it. He shouts at me on the phone. I'm on a team tennis trip, and I put him on speaker.

My friend Tara is next me on the hotel bed. She laughs and says, "This is so crazy. This guy is literally in our biology class." Dick gets angrier. I tell him he's being possessive, that it's over. And then we break up.

We break up again the day he follows me around a Halloween party like a little puppy, and the afternoon he throws a fit over wanting to see deleted photos on my phone, and the night he chases me through an apartment complex with a pair of scissors.

This happens near the end of the fall semester, when we're at Dick's old apartment partying with the hockey boys. One of them is Dick's brother-in-law Ben. I'm talking to Ben while Dick plays beer pong. Dick sees me and Ben sitting in the corner of the living room and leaves the party in a jealous rage. I don't even realize what's happened until I look at my phone and see a text from him that reads, "Fuck you."

Ben and I were talking about Dick. I was lying about how good our relationship was. There's nothing flirty between us. I'm not even attracted to Ben.

I go looking for Dick. He's at his new apartment a two-minute walk away. When I get there, he says I'm a whore, that I was flirting with his brother-in-law because I flirt with everybody. He grabs a pair of scissors and starts cutting his wrists. I sprint into the grass between the apartments, terrified that the scissors are coming for me next. Dick is behind me. I run toward the hockey party, because it's dark out and I know people are there. The whole time, Dick's chasing me and screaming, "Mayci, stop, stop. Mayci, come here!" I don't look back. I have no idea if he still has the scissors.

When I get back to the party, I run straight to the biggest bedroom, where I hide in the closet. I didn't realize the guy who rents that room lets his dog poop there. So I'm sitting on the floor, shaking, surrounded by piles of dog shit. I call Dick's sister and tell her what's happening, then hear shouting. The closet door bursts open and Dick grabs me. He doesn't have the scissors anymore, but he looks furious.

"Don't touch me!" I scream, recoiling. "Let me go!"

Ben comes in and stands up for me. I'm surprised—Dick is a big guy. People usually let him get his way. This is the first time someone has defended me.

I tell Ben that Dick was trying to hurt me.

"She's drunk," Dick says. "She doesn't know what she's talking about." He says I'm lying and out of my mind. Ben doesn't buy it. He can see how scared I am. He kicks Dick out of the party.

BYU DOESN'T HAVE AN amnesty policy. I know that if I report Dick for abusing me, I'll get in trouble, too, because I've been drinking. These days, things are different. If you report something, there aren't the same kinds of penalties. But in 2013, I know I can't go to the school for help. And Dick does too. He weaponizes the honor code against me again and again. Each time I break up with him, he says he'll report me, so each time I break up with him, I have to take him back.

I START TO DRINK more. I know I shouldn't party this much. But I can't stop. Each time I cross a line, I feel like I might as well do it again. Drinking, partying, oral sex: it all feels horrible the first time, and then it's like I'm numb to it.

One night, when I'm drunk and hanging out at Dick's apartment, I fall into his door. It's broken already, partially coming off its hinges. When I collapse into it, it comes all the way off.

It should be funny, but Dick screams, "What the fuck are you doing? You're so fucking stupid. What's wrong with you? You're a fucking idiot!"

Sam and his girlfriend are there. They watch this and say nothing. Dick storms out. He likes to drive drunk to scare us. It's a threat and an attempt to get my attention.

The whole time he's gone, the three of us panic. I imagine Dick killing someone or himself. When he finally comes back and idles in his car outside, I say I want to leave. I want to go home.

From his car, Dick sees us walk out of the apartment and get into Sam's car. He climbs out of the driver's seat and says, "You guys aren't leaving."

"Let's go," I say to Sam.

We try to reverse, but Dick runs to the other side, blocking us.

I say, "Sam, please, let's go."

But Sam doesn't protect me; he doesn't know what to do. When Dick tells him to unlock the doors, he does, letting Dick into the car. Dick takes the seat next to me in back. He starts grabbing my chest under my shirt. I say, "Don't touch me." He keeps going. He puts his hands down my pants. "Stop touching me," I say again. Later that night, Dick assaults me in his room. He doesn't take my virginity, but he does things that scar me and leave me feeling ashamed to this day; things I still haven't told my husband or therapist about; things that shouldn't happen to anybody.

TWELVE

ONE OF OUR BREAKUPS LASTS A LITTLE LONGER: ALMOST a month. I hear Dick is seeing someone else. I feel slightly jealous, but relieved at the same time. I get drunk and go to a party at Dick's old apartment with the hockey boys. My friend Nicole, who I know from Southern California and the tennis team, comes with me. Dick's brother-in-law Ben is there. I'm still not attracted to him. But ever since he's saved me from Dick, I have this weird guilt complex around him. I feel like I owe him.

A group of us starts playing card games. Everyone else is drinking beer, but I go for shots. I'm a broken person at this point. I honestly feel like Dick has ruined me. I haven't done anything with other guys except make out, but I still feel like a slut, and when Dick shows up unexpectedly, I start crying. None of the hockey guys want him there. They're afraid of him too. I feel like everyone knows he's crazy. A loose cannon.

Dick tells me that I'm drunk and that he wants to take me home so he can take care of me. I say, "You're seeing someone else." He keeps trying to get me to leave the apartment with him. I tell him to get away from me. The guys intervene. They stand between us. One of them says, "She doesn't want to go with you," then pulls me into a bedroom so I can decompress. When we're in there, the guy leans in and kisses me. I'm so drunk that I kiss him back. I don't even know if I want to. Dick opens the bedroom door. As the handle turns, the guy and I jump apart. I don't know what exactly Dick sees.

I know I'm acting like a slut. But I feel powerful. All these guys want me. And Dick knows it. He sees what he's missing. I yell at him to "get the fuck out," and he leaves the apartment, furious. Nicole comes into the bedroom with Dick's brother-in-law Ben and two other guys. She starts making out with one of them. I kiss Ben. I don't know why I do it. I know I would never make out with Ben or any of these hockey guys while sober. But I'm not sober. I'm drunk and angry and I want to do something destructive.

While Ben's at my lips, another guy starts kissing my neck. None of us do more than kiss, but it's my wildest night yet. The next morning, I'm overcome with shame and regret. I don't even know who I am anymore.

I GET BACK TOGETHER with Dick a week later, mainly because of the guilt I feel over kissing three of his teammates. But he keeps asking me what happened that night. I deny that I hooked up with any of the hockey guys because I'm afraid of him. I don't trust him not to hurt himself or choke me again. He starts to ask me about that night every day. I keep saying nothing happened.

One day, we're at my sister's house cuddling on the couch. She's in California.

Dick says, "Tell me the truth about that night. I swear I won't be mad. I promise. Just tell me."

I do, with tears in my eyes, and he goes ballistic.

He's crying and screaming, "You're a fucking slut, Mayci! You're a fucking whore!" He stands up and goes into my sister's kitchen. Nobody else is home. He screams that he's going to report me for breaking the BYU honor code. "You're fucked, you're all fucked!" he shouts. "I'm turning all of you in."

I beg him to calm down. He reaches for a ten-inch butcher knife and walks toward me. He says, "You deserve to feel pain like I do right now."

I don't remember what happens next. My next memory is him storming out the front door and slipping on my sister's steps. It's been snowing. As he falls, his face slams into the frozen pavement. His nose bleeds, the red drops blossoming in the snow.

TOLD YOU SO

When he stands up, he looks pathetic and terrifying. I help him inside, leading him to the bathroom and gathering toilet paper for his nose. It's a half bath, and we're cramped inside trying to stop the bleeding. He's standing in front of the mirror, sobbing and saying, "I can't believe you would do this to me."

I don't remember how I get him to leave. I stay at my sister's house. I feel sick to my stomach; like a little kid. I can't leave him or I'll lose everything. My scholarship, my spot on the tennis team, my chance to start a life outside my parents' house.

But I know I can't stay with him either. I pace the living room and kitchen, unsure how to tell anyone what happened. I've broken the honor code so many times. Dick has pictures of me drinking, of me topless, of me smoking. I'm terrified he'll turn them in. And I'm afraid he's going to hurt those guys I made out with. He's said he's going to "make them bite the fucking curb." I don't want it to be my fault anyone is hurt.

Thirty minutes later, I get a text from him saying he's suicidal. If he dies, he says, it's my fault, so I better get to his apartment ASAP. I drive to his apartment, where he binge-drinks and snorts crushed-up prescription pills from the box he keeps locked in his apartment. I assume it holds the meds he was prescribed but doesn't take. I sit on his bed, shaking and trapped. Between each line, he looks over at me and says, "See what you've made me do, Mayci?"

THIRTEEN

I GET A MINOR BREAK FROM DICK WHEN I'M HOME FOR THE holidays. We're both back in Southern California to visit our families. He can't get to me as much when I'm living with my parents, but on New Year's, we go to a party together, where he accuses me of flirting with his uncle and drunkenly screams at me the whole drive home. When I return to school in January, things between us are worse. I'm still a virgin, and I want to keep it that way, but Dick clearly wants to have sex. It's a relief that it's tennis season now. I'll be traveling more.

Our first in-season match is in Oklahoma. Lauren and I take a picture under the time clock wearing our matching Nike Dri-FIT shirts with "Jones" printed across the back.

Oklahoma tried to recruit me, and I'm eager to show them what they missed out on. But I play poorly and lose. Afterward, our team listens to "Timber," which has just come out, in the minivan. My sister is driving.

She says, "That was embarrassing. That was bad. We literally got timbered."

Everyone laughs, including me. I wasn't expecting Oklahoma's players to be as good as they were. I can't believe how much I lost by. I feel embarrassed for myself and bad for Lauren. If I'm not winning, it reflects poorly on her.

TWO WEEKS LATER, DURING one of my matches, Lauren asks why I'm so mad. We're standing on the corner of the court, in Idaho or San Francisco or Virginia. I tell her that I want to be riled up. I want to be mad. She doesn't get it. I tell her I don't want to be told where to hit in a calm, soft voice. I want someone to get angry with me, to say, "You're so much better than her, you should be winning easily," and if my opponent is cheating, "That girl's a bitch. She's cheating. Don't let her cheat you." I want tough love.

At my next match, our assistant coach stands on my court. He says, "No excuses. Hit harder." I win the match but don't celebrate. I feel like I have to win every game. That's the expectation. Winning isn't something to celebrate; it's a box to check. I play when I'm exhausted, when I'm traumatized, when I have the stomach flu. If I can't go out on the court because something's wrong with me, everyone has to shift up, so it's harder for the team to win.

I start to hurt myself on the court. I pound my legs with my racket until they're covered in bruises. I've always been competitive, but I've never been much of a yeller. I'm a chill person. But Dick makes everything a fight, and after a year with him, I become someone who shouts and swears.

DICK FINDS WAYS TO torture me about tennis. When I'm practicing on campus, he drives by the outdoor court in his souped-up Mustang and revs the engine. He knows I'll know it's him; the sound is unmistakable. Before matches, he tells me to hurry up and lose so I can come party with him.

During one match, he stands at the very edge of my court, his face pressed against the fence. Each time I serve, he tries to talk to me.

You're not allowed to speak to a player during a match unless you're their coach. It's distracting. My mom, who's been traveling with our team as a nanny for Lauren's daughter Presley, goes over to him.

She says, "You can't stand this close to her."

He backs off a little bit, but I can tell he's pissed. He doesn't want my parents telling him anything. Now that he's gotten me away from them, he feels like I'm his.

A couple days later, when we're driving, I tell him I leg-pressed 450 pounds. I'm really proud of myself. He turns to me with this awful expression on his face and says, "Wow, I'm Mayci Fucking Jones. I leg-pressed four hundred fifty pounds."

FOURTEEN

I'M AT ASU PLAYING A GIRL FROM THE UNIVERSITY OF MICHigan. A lot of teams don't want to play at BYU because we're at altitude, so Lauren has us doing a series of matches in Arizona. The girl is good, and I should be enjoying the match. But I'm pissed off. I can't stop swearing on the court. The line judges are coding me.

Lauren tells me to keep my cool. Tennis is a quiet sport, but I'm smashing my racket against my leg and screaming. It looks bad for Lauren, and it looks bad for BYU.

There's a tiebreaker. The match comes down to the final set. I'm up 6–4. I miss an easy short ball I should've been able to put away for the win, and I scream and throw my racket on the court.

Afterward, Lauren can tell I'm not in a normal headspace. She says I'm either totally different than she thought, or something really bad is happening with me.

SOMETHING REALLY BAD *IS* happening with me. But I can't ask for help. I briefly think about going to a bishop and repenting. I know there's a chance I could talk to someone kind—someone who wants to work on things with me. Or I could get someone who turns me in for breaking the honor code and takes away my scholarship and makes me leave school, which would embarrass my entire family. I can't risk that.

But I'm terrified. One night, Dick gets pissed off for no reason and says he's going to drive drunk. This has become one of his go-to moves. He stands at his front door holding his keys. I reach for his arm to keep him from leaving. He pushes me, but I reach out again, begging him not to leave. He shoves me into the door. Hard. The metal hinge slices my heel open. Blood pours from my Achilles onto the floor. It squirts up to my calf.

I say, "Look what you did."

I'm in season. What if I'm actually injured?

Dick says he's mad at himself and starts hitting himself in the face. I hold his wrists down to stop him, and eventually he moves to the bed, where he dozes off.

I try to leave, but each time I get up, he stirs and asks me to stay. I look at the black decal of the tree on his wall. Each leaf is stuck on individually. I stare at it and think about calling the cops. I want someone to come and save me. But I've had a few drinks and I'm afraid the cops will give me a citation. If that happens, BYU will find out and I'll get an honor code violation. Then I'll get kicked out of school, and all of the hiding will have been for nothing.

When Dick is finally in a deep sleep, I text Meghan, from the tennis team, and ask her to come get me. It's six a.m. I haven't slept for a second. Meghan comes around seven when she sees the text. I tiptoe out to her car, terrified.

I don't tell her I thought Dick was going to kill me, although for a moment I did. I say we got in a fight and I was uncomfortable. And later, when I get my heel taped by the trainer so I can play tennis at practice, I don't tell the truth about what happened to it. I just say I tripped into the doorjamb.

ANOTHER NIGHT AT HIS apartment, Dick he says he's going to make us drinks. I don't watch him make mine. I remember him handing it to me. I remember sipping it. And then I remember him naked on top of me while I say, "I don't want to, I don't want to," over and over again. I remember the feeling of trying to scream but having no voice. Everything is hazy. I can't keep my eyes open no matter how hard I try.

The next morning, he says, "I can't believe that happened."

We're in the car driving to breakfast.

"What happened?" I ask.

He tells me we had sex. I say we didn't. He says we did. He gets mad at me for not remembering our first time. I stare out the car window. I have no idea what he's talking about until I start to recall flashes of the night. It makes me feel sick.

When we park, I have no appetite. We get our food to go. I can't even eat it.

Later in the day, I go to Lauren's house, where I play with Presley, who's not even one yet. I can't believe I'm living these two different lives.

When I get back to Dick's apartment that night, he offers me shots to loosen me up. He wants to have sex again to "spark my memory." I know he assaulted me. But I can't bear to let myself think of it as rape. I've always thought of rape as someone hiding in the bushes, jumping out, and grabbing you. It's hard for me to define what Dick did, but I know it's wrong.

I take two shots and reluctantly have sex with him again, even though I don't want to. While he's moving over me, I feel completely disassociated. I understand that he's won and I've lost. All I had left was my virginity, and he's cheated and taken it. I'm furious at myself, and embarrassed for not listening to my parents. When Dick finishes, I tell him I love him, because if I can convince myself I do, then all of this is a little less awful; then I'm a little less trapped.

FIFTEEN

I FIND A MEME OF A GIRL WHOSE FACE IS COVERED IN bruises. The text reads, "She better say she fell down the stairs if she knows what's good for her."

I show this to my friend Tara and say, "Isn't this funny?"

She's like, "Mayci, no."

I'm laughing. I tell her it's hilarious. I can tell she's wondering if I'm OK. I'm not, but I tell her I'm all good; I just have a dark sense of humor.

I can't open up to anyone. I wouldn't even know where to start. I've done so many things I'm ashamed of. There's the sex, the drugs, and the drinking. But there's also the manipulation. A part of me knows I need to get out—and I know anyone would tell me I need that too. But I'm in too deep.

Dick wants to have sex constantly now. I'm only safe when I'm traveling for tennis. The trips are never long enough.

In Boise, where I'm playing the Broncos, the matches are held indoors because of snow. I lose my singles match 5–7, 6–4, 10–6. Close. In doubles, Nicole and I win. The team wins too.

That night, my mom, who's been traveling with the team to take care of Presley, sees me texting Dick. She doesn't know about the abuse, but she knows he's bad news. My whole family has wanted me to break up with him since I got to BYU. As they've seen me disappear into his world, they want it even more.

My mom tells my dad I'm still talking to Dick, and my dad calls me. I'm relaxing in my hotel room when I pick up. He asks me to go into the hall.

I do, and he starts screaming into the receiver. "If you don't break up with this fucking asshole," he shouts, "I'm going to fucking fly down there!" When my mom is pissed, I don't really care, because I'm so used to her getting mad. But my dad never yells at me. I'm scared shitless by his anger. I have no idea how to deal with it. And I know I don't have a leg to stand on. He's obviously right. "You need to break up with him now," he continues.

"OK," I say. "I will."

But I know I can't. I'm worried Dick will retaliate if I leave him. And if I tell my parents what's going on, they'll drag me home. I'm trapped by the combination of my Mormon values, which make me feel like I have to love him, and by his seeming blackmail.

I DECIDE TO HIDE my relationship with Dick. We start to talk over Facebook Messenger because my dad says he has access to my texts. I still spend almost every night at Dick's apartment. But nothing about our relationship is fun anymore.

My birthday is on a Saturday that year. I know Dick's not going to do anything big for it, but my friends do. They throw me a full-on surprise party. They've made me a cake with a drawing of a tennis racket and a ball made of frosting. It's fun and special. I feel loved. I want to stay as long as possible, but Dick tells me we should leave early. I push back—it's my birthday party!—and we get in a fight. Dick basically hauls me home. I'm teetering on the frozen sidewalk in my heels. When we get back to Dick's apartment, it's clear he only wanted to leave early to have sex. I have no interest, but we do it anyway. It's the first time we've done it without a condom. I don't know how hard it can be to get pregnant. I don't know anything about semen or ovulation or actual sex ed, so I freak out and ask Dick to get us Plan B even though he didn't finish inside me. We drive to a CVS together the next morning, my actual birthday. I don't want anyone to see me inside, so I ask him to go get it. He does.

When he gets back to the car, he chucks it at me and says, "Happy fucking birthday."

I'M WITH NICOLE AT the Student Athlete Building. That's where I meet Arik for the first time. I don't pay attention to him, really, beyond thinking he's annoying. He seems like a little brother: goofy and fun. We talk a little about partying and smoking weed. He's taller than Dick. And he's wearing a black Marlins baseball hat. I like him, but I don't think about him beyond that. With Dick, I'm not allowed to look at other guys. It's just not worth noticing if anyone is cute, because nothing good can come of it.

Except Dick isn't feeling well. He complains that his stomach hurts. He's had issues for months—he's seen all these specialists and even had an endoscopy, which turned up nothing. I think it's an anxiety disorder. He freaks out every time I'm out of his sight.

He doesn't get better, and in March, he tells me he's leaving BYU to go back to California and figure out what is going on with his stomach. It happens so fast. One second, I'm basically his prisoner, and the next he's standing beside his packed car in the parking lot of the freshman dorms, telling me he's leaving.

He wants to stay together. I tell him we need to break up so I can focus on the rest of the tennis season. I'm overly nice about it. I tell him I love him and that maybe we'll get together in California when I get back. I don't want him to retaliate and turn me in for honor code violations. But I know I can't do this anymore. If he does turn me in, at least that will end it. I'll lose my scholarship, but at least I'll be free.

Dick cries and asks if we can still talk.

I say yes. I'm so confused. I hate him more than I've ever hated anyone, but he's gaslit and manipulated me for so long that I'm more insecure than ever. I watch him climb into his packed car, reverse, and pull out of the lot.

And then he's gone. Suddenly, out of nowhere, I have my life back.

SIXTEEN

I START PLAYING WELL AGAIN. TARA AND I WIN THREE DOUbles matches in a row. I feel so much freer now that Dick isn't waiting for me after every practice. Now that I don't have to go back to his apartment. Now that I don't have to sleep with him or stare at the black tree decal on his wall.

But I still think I see him on campus. I flinch at the sound of a revving engine. And when I lie in bed alone, I relive the night he pulled the knife on me, the night he chased me with scissors, the night he drugged me and took my virginity.

Each morning, I wonder if this is the day he's going to report me. He has videos of us having sex that he took when I was blackout drunk. Pictures of me drinking. A clip of me smoking weed. Before he left, I told him to delete all of them, but I have no idea if he actually did. But the longer I'm on campus without him, the more I feel like myself. *Go ahead and report me*, I start thinking to myself. The distance helps me understand how bad it was and how much worse it could've been. Even if he does report me, I'm just glad to be free.

I start going over to Lauren's house to hang out. I never did that when Dick was in Utah because I was worried Lauren would see how messed up I truly was. But I love hanging out with her, her husband Kirk, and Presley. I missed them. We always have fun at our Sunday dinners: we eat the same thing—grilled chicken and salad—every time.

I reconnect with my friends too. Tara, Nicole, and I drive to Swig. I party on the weekends because it's a habit now. Without Dick on campus, everything is more fun. I can wear my lace crop tops and short skirts. I can be myself. I learn how to have a life without Dick around—without him deciding what I do after every practice and match.

One afternoon, Nicole and I are at the Student Athlete Building when Arik walks over. I immediately clock his bright blue eyes. I don't know how I missed them before. He's wearing a blue BYU hat, which makes his eyes look even brighter. For a moment, I'm like, *What the heck? Is this the same guy?* Arik sits down with us, and we invite him to tag along to Swig. The second we get in the car, I forget that Arik's attractive—because he's *so* annoying. I'm in the front seat. He's in the back. He keeps reaching his hand up to take Snapchats of my double chin. I swat his phone away and wonder why I'm spending any time with him.

But when I run into him the next day, we hang out again. And then again.

Arik is the opposite of Dick. He's goofy, hard to get, fun, carefree, and flirty. He's on the baseball team, so we talk about the pressures of playing tennis and pitching. Neither of us say we're bad Mormons, but it's clear that we're both struggling with the strict guidelines around our faith. We spend our nights sneaking into Jacuzzis at various apartment complexes in Provo. One night, at the Village, Arik offers me alcohol in an insulated water bottle.

I don't like to drink the day before a tennis match.

He says, "One shot."

I'm easy to convince. And Arik is convincing. His energy charms me completely. He makes everyone around him want to have fun and be fun. I take more than one shot. I'm buzzed from the alcohol, from Arik's leg next to mine under the water, from the Jacuzzi's bubbles.

On the drive home that night, we can't stop giggling. We cuddle like a couple, but we don't kiss. I'm surprised by how captivating I find Arik. He's not trolling me anymore. He's fun, hilarious, and relatable. I feel excited about what will happen next.

I GO TO ONE of Arik's baseball games. His shoulder is injured, so we watch together from the stands. I post videos of the game on Snapchat and Instagram, and some of my teammates text to ask if we're dating. I don't know how to answer. What do you say when someone's taking you bowling, sneaking into hot tubs with you, and buying you food, but you still haven't kissed?

Everything feels different with Arik. He's funnier than anyone I've ever dated or even met. And he plays hard to get. I've never dated someone my own age. Mark, Cole, and Dick were all older. With Arik we're totally on the same page. We never talk about having had sex with other people, but we know neither of us is a virgin. Still, nobody makes a move. We're totally chaste. I respond to my teammates, "Haha. No we're not dating!"

ONE DAY, WITH NOTHING better to do, Arik and I drive the twenty minutes to his parents' house. We've only been hanging out for a week or two, but I'm nervous to meet them, because family is everything. But I love them immediately. His mom reminds me a little of mine. Later, Arik tells me his parents haven't liked a lot of girls he's brought home in the past, but his dad likes me because I look him in the eye when I talk to him and because I'm also a D1 athlete. I'm like, *Of course I make eye contact.*

We all go out to eat at Cafe Rio. I feel so awkward about them buying me dinner that I order a kid's quesadilla, which is literally free. It's only one slice. While I'm eating it, I admit to myself that I have a full-on crush on Arik. If I didn't, I wouldn't feel these butterflies in my belly.

That night, we watch a movie in his parents' basement. I'm sure he's going to kiss me. He keeps moving his head toward mine, teasing me, then pulling back.

After an hour, I wonder if maybe he's not into me after all. Maybe he's gay. Or maybe I'm not his type. I'm even more confused when his little brother Jeff Jr., who's three years younger than us and still in high school, comes down and joins us.

Jeff Jr. says he wants to walk to an old haunted house on a nearby hill. Arik tells me it was abandoned after housing a polygamous cult. It's a spooky idea. And I love spooky. We grab coats and go outside, making our way through the neighborhood. The hill is steep. We pant as we push through the overgrown bushes, thorns catching on our jeans.

We stop at a crumbling wall, where someone has drawn a pentagram symbol. I tell Arik I'm scared, and the two of us hold hands.

AFTERWARD, ARIK AND I head back toward BYU. I'm driving, with Arik in the passenger seat. We should go home and get to sleep, but neither of us want to. We speed past the dorms and into the neighborhood above campus. The houses are bigger there, and the roads curve as they climb the mountain. We stop at a turn-off with a view of the entire city. Most nights, cars occupy every spot. We find an empty one facing campus, our backs to Y Mountain. It's March, so there's still snow on the peaks across the lake. I can see temples, the illuminated football field, lights sparkling in the windows of distant houses. It's beautiful. I turn on Spotify. Arik says he doesn't like country. I tell him I used to not like it either. I play him a few songs to try to convince him it's not that bad. The whole time, I'm wondering if he's ever going to kiss me. Finally, during the chorus of "Cowboy Take Me Away," he leans over, grabs my face, and presses his lips against mine. Everything about it is perfect.

SEVENTEEN

ARIK INVITES ME TO HIS FAMILY-ONLY BIRTHDAY PARTY. We've only been hanging out for a couple weeks, but it feels totally normal for me to accompany his parents and brother to a Brazilian restaurant in Provo. The food is good, and I can't help but notice it's expensive. It's a restaurant people in Provo go to for special occasions.

After dinner, Arik asks his mom to take a couple of pictures of us. I'm wearing a black spaghetti-strap top, skinny jeans, and a cardigan. I'm too embarrassed to actually sit on Arik's lap for the photo—I don't want his mom to get the wrong idea or think I'm provocative—so I sort of squat over him, my quads shaking.

That weekend, we go to a baseball party. Arik and I get drunk and stumble to an upstairs area with a putt-putt course, where we lay down, hold hands, and take a Snapchat. We're both holding Swig cups filled with alcohol: it's my trick so I don't get caught breaking the honor code. I don't know the baseball guys enough to trust them not to report me, so I need to be subtle about drinking around them. There's no way to be sure that no one will snitch. I know people who have been caught because someone sent pictures of them drinking to the dean of students.

Arik and I move to the couch, still holding our Swig cups. That's the last thing I remember. I wake up in a room I've never seen before and freak out, thinking I've been kidnapped. I legitimately think someone has abducted me. I can see a wooden dresser and a TV. My bracelet—black and gold and chunky—is wrapped around the TV's power cord. My clothes are scattered all over the floor. I turn and see Arik. That makes me feel better, until I realize I'm naked. I immediately think I'm a slut. I had sex with someone I've only known for a few weeks. I start to panic.

I'm Mormon! I don't do this stuff!

I wake Arik and awkwardly laugh, then say, "Ugh I'm naked?"

He says, "Huh?" and rubs a hand across his sleepy eyes.

Neither of us can remember if we had sex. Both of us have basically no memories of the night. But we're happy to be waking up together. He tells me we're in one of the rooms at the baseball house. We leave and I meet up with my mom, who's in town. She and I get dinner with my brother Alex in Salt Lake City. I spend the whole meal reliving the night. I have a vague memory of lying naked underneath Arik and him asking, "Have you done this before?"

I decide it's funny that Arik and I blacked out in a stranger's room. I know he didn't take advantage of me. I know he's a really good guy. But just in case we had sex, I want Plan B.

I text Arik. He's convinced we didn't have sex, and I truly don't think we did either, but I make him get me Plan B, and when we meet up later that night, I take it. I'm not risking anything.

I NEVER LET DICK into my dorm room. I never wanted him there. But after three weeks of hanging out, Arik starts coming over almost every day and sleeping over almost every night. At BYU, no boys are allowed inside the girls' dorms after nine p.m. and vice versa.

To sneak in, Arik pulls his hood over his face, and we howl with laughter as we race up to my hall. I go to the vending machines to score us some Hot Pockets to heat up in my microwave. My roommate has moved out, so we have the place to ourselves. We don't have sex. We just hang out and talk.

It's crazy how comfortable I am with Arik. He's from Utah. Nicole told me that his family has money, but it's hard to believe, because he doesn't show it. He dresses badly: in cargo shorts I swear I've seen in my dad's closet. He almost always wears a hat.

I like that he's not pretentious. And I have a feeling that things haven't just been handed to him. We talk about almost everything: I don't say a lot about Dick, and he doesn't go on and on about his ex, who he's recently broken up with. But we touch on our pasts. We tease each other. And we have so much fun. Arik makes me feel invincible. He starts to pull me out of my dark place.

That doesn't mean we're not reckless. I start to black out every time we drink. It helps me push away the trauma from everything with Dick. And it lets me have fun.

I feel safe with Arik. But I also feel like a slut. And I can only dim my memories of Dick so much. I still resent him for stealing my virginity, and I'm afraid that now that I've messed around with two people, nobody's going to want me.

At least I'm still playing good tennis. I play San Diego and beat Shani Blecher 6–2, 6–2, with Arik watching in the stands, then win against Gonzaga's Kylie Peek 6–0, 6–3. It's nice to have the guy I'm seeing support me and act like a normal, caring person.

ONE WEEKEND WHEN I don't have tennis, I drive Arik to the BYU volleyball house. It's not on-campus housing, which means it's a good place to party. I say I'm not drinking because I'm driving, then have a screwdriver. It tastes so good I have another. The next thing I remember is making out with Arik in the laundry room on top of the washing machine, and again in the bathroom, knocking the towels all over the floor. I've never felt so much passion with anyone.

To this day, I have no idea how we get home.

When I wake up at four in the morning, Arik and I are in my twin bed. I don't remember sneaking him into my dorm, but I do have a faint memory of us having sex and then wobbling down the hall to pee. I'm paranoid of getting a UTI, since I've heard stories from my mom and sisters.

When I come back to my room, Arik is asleep. I get into the other bed.

He wakes up briefly and asks if I want to cuddle with him. I say no. I'm too drunk and tired to get up again.

The next time I wake, Arik's gone. There's loose change on the floor. My wallet and car keys are missing. I call him, panicking. No answer.

I spend an hour looking for my keys. I know I must have them somewhere, because I needed them to get into my dorm, but they've disappeared. I call Arik again, and he doesn't answer again. Then I prop my door open with the deadbolt and walk out to the parking lot, where I find my keys and wallet on the front seat of my unlocked car. I have no idea how they got there.

EIGHTEEN

I CHECK MY PHONE AND FIND FIVE MISSED CALLS FROM ARIK. He's texted too.

"Call me, something bad just happened."

When I call him back from the Chick-fil-A on campus, he doesn't answer. I assume he's in trouble about the BYU honor code, meaning I'm probably in trouble about the BYU honor code. I'm so anxious I feel like my stomach is falling out of my ass.

I call him again, my hands shaking, then drive back to my dorm. I imagine my parents driving to BYU to pick me up, Lauren's face as I clean out my locker.

When Arik finally calls me later that night, he says there's no problem with the honor code. Instead, his parents are mad because they know we spent the night at their house when they were out of town. Also, his ex-girlfriend thinks she might be pregnant.

My first thought is how relieved I am to not be the one who's pregnant or in trouble with the honor code.

ARIK AND I MEET up later that night. Neither of us is too worried about the ex. We both assume it's a ploy to win Arik back. The thing with his parents isn't that bad either. We were sober that night and only made out. We just didn't want to have to sneak into the dorms. When I think about it, I realize we haven't done anything that bad at all. I can't even feel guilty about it.

Arik's been taking a bowling class at BYU, so we go bowling. He teaches me how to throw with my arm straight instead of hurling the ball as hard as I can. I like that we always do activities together: bowling or mini golf or going to the movies. I reassure him that his parents will get over their disappointment. It's all going to be fine.

SCHOOL ENDS A FEW days later. I don't study as hard as I should. I get in line late for all my exams, which means I spend hours waiting around at the testing center.

But I'm not worried. I'm at BYU to be a tennis player, and after that, I'll be a stay-at-home mom. My grades don't matter at all.

When the dorms close for the summer, I move into Lauren's house twenty minutes from campus and Arik goes home to Spanish Fork. We hang out my last night in Utah. We don't have a tearful goodbye. It's been a really fun month—maybe the most fun month of my life—but we never defined the relationship. No labels. No rules. I tell him I'll probably see him later that summer, when I come back to Utah for our tennis team's European tour, and then I go home to California.

I'm sad to leave Arik. But I know neither of us is in a place to date anyone seriously. Dick only left BYU two months ago. It's too soon.

IT'S ISOLATING TO BE in my childhood bedroom again. It feels smaller than before, somehow, and oddly unfamiliar. I miss sneaking into Jacuzzis with Arik. I miss lying in his arms. And I hate the way my parents want to know where I'm going all the time. Why do they care so much? I'm not a little girl anymore.

When I get my GPA for the semester, it's a 1.9. My parents are like, *Seriously?* But no one actually cares. I'm a communications major because I'm vaguely interested in broadcast journalism, but everyone knows I'm never going to have a real job. Women in my family traditionally get married and raise a family. If we do get a job, it's going back to our roots, aka teaching tennis part-time. I have a dream of doing some kind of internship in a big city like New York or London, but I know I don't want to work forever.

ARIK AND I TEXT a lot at the beginning of the summer, but eventually, our communication fizzles out. I start having fun in California. I go to the movies with friends and sneak vodka in my Slurpee. I occasionally smoke weed at the beach. One weekend, I go down to the University of San Diego to see a guy I met at a BYU party who plays on the San Diego volleyball team. I tell my parents I'm spending the weekend with a girlfriend, Molly, who goes to BYU and lives in San Diego, and me, Molly, and the guy meet up at an apartment.

It's weird to be hanging out with UCSD students. At BYU, you have to hide your drinks. Here, people are drinking and taking pictures and videos of themselves partying. I'm like, *This is crazy*. I wish I could text Arik about it. Instead, I get hammered with Molly, then climb into a car with her and some guys to drive to a party at an on-campus bar. I'm so drunk I don't notice the car stopping, or the police lights, or the door opening. But when an officer shines his flashlight in my face, I realize something is wrong and I sober up immediately.

He asks us all to get out of the car, then turns his back to write the driver a ticket. We're parked on the edge of campus, where there's a wooded area. I decide to run for it. I can't get a ticket. I'm on scholarship. I ditch Molly and sprint through the woods until I see people. I've reached the party. I find Molly there. She tells me she sprinted away from the cop too. The volleyball player I'm seeing is there, and we all drink more. We end the night at some guy's apartment. I'm ready to go back to Molly's place, but we don't have a car. And neither of us should be driving anyway.

I'm not drunk enough to have sex, or do anything physical for that matter, so I talk to the volleyball player for hours. He has a perfect body, including a chiseled six-pack. But I don't mess around unless I'm basically blackout.

My sober mind usually makes goodish decisions. And I can't help but think about Arik. He's my favorite person to party with, the person I feel safest with.

BACK HOME, I STARE at my phone, hoping Arik will text me. I think about reaching out to him, but I don't want to seem clingy. I read through our old flirty messages, insecure because I haven't heard from him, then I think about texting Dick. I know it's crazy, but I feel afraid nobody will ever love me the way he did. I have Stockholm syndrome—Dick and I trauma-bonded so much it's hard to fully let go.

Against my better judgment, I text him. I ask if we should just hook up with no strings attached. He responds, "I bet you have a line of guys waiting to fuck you," and I think, *You know what, I do.* I'm so grateful I don't follow through.

I FLY BACK TO Utah to meet the tennis team. We're going to Europe to compete. I'm in the terminal when I see Arik's posted a Snapchat that says "Life is going to change."

I haven't asked him if his ex is pregnant, but I assume this means she is. I click over to her page. There's an Instagram video of a doppler and a caption that reads, "Little heartbeat." I knew something was up, but I still feel a knot in my stomach.

I tell my friends, then text him, "Hey, I feel like you've been MIA and I assume it's because your ex-girlfriend's pregnant." I tell him that I hope he's doing OK and that I am there for him as a friend.

He responds right away. He says he didn't know how to tell me. He says he really likes me and cares about me and hasn't known how to navigate all of this. He's worried I'll think he has "baggage" now. I tell him we'll be friends. I don't say we can date, because I'm truly not trying to be a stepmom at nineteen.

ARIK AND I TALK every day when I'm in Europe. I'm afraid of getting charged too much for texting internationally, so I tell him to download WhatsApp.

Our tennis matches are secondary to sightseeing, which is good because the courts are different over there. I slip on the red clay each time I play. I have to line up my swing while my opponent is finishing theirs because I'm not used to sliding on the court on purpose. I'm also rusty, because I've spent my summer smoking and drinking spiked Slurpees. I'm relieved to be mostly playing doubles. At BYU, I play both. If I had to play singles in France, I'd need fifteen inhalers.

Nobody parties on the Europe trip. We've all heard the horror stories of other BYU students who drink on their European tours and end up getting kicked out. There's no time to party anyway. Lauren's made an incredible itinerary. The trip is perfect. My only complaint is the slow walkers and how hard it is to keep track of a huge group of people.

I'M EXCITED TO SEE Arik when I get back to Utah, where I'm staying for a few days before heading back to Orange County. But I've just taken my lash extensions off and I haven't had time to get a fill, so my eyelashes are stumpy and uneven, which makes me feel insecure. Arik doesn't care. He takes me go-karting at an arcade, where we run around like kids. Then we drive over to his parents' house so we can use their pool.

While we're in the water, his parents come out and spend time with us. None of us talk about the fact that Arik's ex is pregnant and that he's had to leave BYU and enroll at Salt Lake Community College. It's the elephant in the room.

When it gets dark, Arik and I drive to Provo, where we order Mexican food with friends. I feel so free. I missed him.

Eventually, the crowd thins until it's just me, Arik, and a couple of guys. We go to a lookout point where we hotbox the car. I get paranoid that someone's going to catch us. We're in a public area. Arik keeps trolling me and saying he sees cops.

All I can think is, *Goodbye, scholarship.*

The night ends at Nicole's apartment, where I crash in an extra bed. Arik joins me, but we don't have sex. We haven't even kissed since the semester ended. We're just flirty friends. I'm tempted to be more, but I'm still not trying to be a stepmom.

NINETEEN

ARIK AND I BECOME A COUPLE THE DAY BEFORE MY DAD'S birthday, which will thrill him when he reads this. I'm in Utah again, this time to work BYU summer tennis camps. Arik tells me he's not in town. I'm disappointed, but when I go over to a friend's place to hang out, she opens the garage, and Arik is standing there holding a dozen red roses. I've wondered how much he cares about me. I've worried I'm the one with stronger feelings. But when I see him standing in the garage with a huge, goofy smile on his face, I know instantly that we both want to see if we can make this work.

We get drunk and have a heart-to-heart. I tell him, "The whole time we've been talking I've been thinking about how much I want you." One thing leads to another, and we have sex, but afterward, I feel anxious. There's so much going on with his ex being pregnant. And it seems annoying to have to drive thirty-five minutes to West Jordan to see him now that he's been kicked out of BYU for breaking the honor code. Still, the heart wants what it wants. Arik is my favorite person—the person who makes me feel the most alive. What's the worst thing that can happen if we give this a shot?

THAT FALL, I LIVE in an apartment. It's better than the dorms. There's a bathroom in my unit, and I can cook quesadillas and sandwiches in the kitchen. I can even have guys over, as long as my roommates don't report me for honor code infractions.

I mostly trust them. But the BYU culture rewards watching and reporting on your fellow students in a way that makes me uncomfortable, and sometimes, the shame I feel about having sex or messing around morphs into paranoia, so I'm not sure if I'm worried about getting caught or just feeling guilty about what I've done.

It's easier to hang out in West Jordan. Arik and I don't have to worry about someone reporting me for honor code violations when we're not in Provo. We don't have to worry about someone hearing us messing around. His roommates don't care.

I'M AT ARIK'S APARTMENT when he tells me he loves me. It's September 2—the night before BYU starts for the fall semester—and we're lying in bed. He turns to me and says, "Guess what?"

I say, "What?"

He cracks a joke. He does this over and over again until it's three a.m. and I know I need to leave to drive home. "Guess what?" he asks again.

"What?"

His voice changes as he says it. He loves me. I tell him I love him too.

TWENTY

I'M HAPPY WITH ARIK, BUT I'M NOT ACTUALLY OK. I'M STILL battling my demons from my time with Dick. Some nights, when Arik is busy, I go for long walks alone in the sketchiest parts of Provo. I almost want something bad to happen to me because I feel like I deserve it and that nobody will care.

One night, after a week of doing this a few times, Arik gives me his dog tag: he tells me he wants me to engrave it for him.

I say, "Engrave it with what?"

He tells me, "I just want you to do it."

The baseball boys all wear special dog tags. It's basically a rite of passage for them. I don't want to mess Arik's up by engraving something stupid. It's a lot of pressure.

But in the end, I decide on the three most important dates in our relationship: the day we had our first kiss, the day we started dating, and the day we said "I love you."

AT A PARTY, I get completely hammered by mixing rum and vodka and taking far too many Jell-O shots. I remember being shoulder to shoulder with people in the living room. I remember doing shots. I remember laughing with Arik at my side. And I remember throwing up in Nicole's bathroom, my knees on the cold floor.

When Arik comes in to see if I'm OK and to check if he can help me, I yell at him. I'm holding the toilet, my hair caked in vomit.

I look at him in the doorway and shout, "Get the fuck out of here!"

I'm so embarrassed he's seen me that vulnerable.

He goes back into the hall. I lock the door and turn on the shower, then black out. When Meghan breaks down the door later, she finds me lying face down in the water. My cheek is pressed against the drain. I'm naked. She thinks I'm dead.

I come to, cradling my knees, and tell her, "I'm alive."

I DON'T STOP DRINKING. I push and push. Other girls have two sips of beer and say they're drunk. I pound drinks until I can't see straight or remember anything.

Like everything else, sex feels less problematic when I'm drinking. It's almost like it's not me doing it. When I'm drunk, I'm not attached. I'm not exposed or vulnerable or sinning. When I'm sober, all the shame and guilt comes roaring back.

I never cry in front of Arik, but that's mostly because I basically don't cry at all. I bottle everything up, funnel it into anger, and let it out on the tennis court.

But sometimes, when I'm really drunk, I open up. One morning, when Arik and I are hungover in his apartment, I have a hazy flashback of sobbing the night before.

I turn to Arik and say, "Did I cry last night?"

It's so embarrassing. I think of crying as a weakness. I can't imagine being that open in front of anyone. It's just not who I am. It doesn't occur to me that the alcohol is exposing a side of me I've been trying to keep hidden.

Arik and I don't talk about how hard it is for me to have sex sober, but I tell him a little bit about the abuse I've experienced. I don't give him every detail, but I tell him how hard it was for me. And I tell him I feel like I'm failing as a Mormon, as a daughter, and as a tennis player. I cry during this conversation, and he does too—because he feels similarly about his own life.

TOLD YOU SO

It surprises both of us. Neither of us is usually emotional.

When I hear from my friend Sam that Dick is back in Provo, I'm terrified of running into him. I know he's not back at school. But I don't even want him in Utah.

One night, he calls and leaves a voicemail. My voicemail inbox is broken, so I can't actually listen to it, but the whole thing really freaks me out. I jump at the littlest sound; I flinch when I see someone who looks like him. It's a relief to have a night of driving around Utah and laughing with Arik. Everything feels easy with him, as long as I don't think about his pregnant ex-girlfriend.

TWENTY-ONE

THE LONGER I DATE ARIK, THE LESS COMPLICATED SEX feels. I don't spend as much time thinking about Dick, which means I'm not as easily triggered. And I realize sex can actually be enjoyable. I can even joke about it. Arik and I will be hanging out with friends and one of us will say "Peaches," which means we want to have sex. Sometimes, we'll even yell it across a room.

I wish I could tell my parents about how much fun I'm having. How much better this fall semester is than the last one. I'd never mention the sex, because they'd drag me home. But I want to share Arik. I know if they understood how wonderful he is, they'd be happy for me. And if they knew how truly horrible my last relationship was, they'd be grateful I'm with him. But I can't tell them about all my trauma with Dick. And Arik's situation is complicated. My parents won't want me dating another bad boy—they won't want me with someone whose ex is pregnant, or someone who had to leave BYU—even one who's helped me so much with everything.

THE ONE TIME I tell my parents the truth about my love life is when I see Liam for the first time. He's a football player: a new transfer to BYU from Oregon. I lock eyes with him in the Student Athlete Building. He's completely gorgeous.

We don't talk to each other, but I turn to Nicole and say, "Who the hell is that?" Nicole tells me his name is Liam. I've never been so physically attracted to someone. I tell her, "That's my future husband." It's what I tell my parents on the phone that night too.

A few days later, there's a party at the Village apartments. It's one of the nicer complexes near campus. The buildings are new. They have a soda shop downstairs. I'm not planning on going. But everyone knows I think Liam is hot, and one of my friends texts me to say Liam is there. I get there in record time. Arik can't hang out that night because he says he has a baseball bonding activity. I don't think flirting with Liam counts as cheating—or at least I tell myself that.

There's never parking at the Village, but I find a spot right in front. It feels like it's meant to be. Inside, I make a point of not going up to Liam. My vibe is that he'll notice me, and I have too much of an ego to ever go up to a man first. I dance with my friend Tara while making sure Liam sees me.

When the party ends, I talk to all these guys on my way out. I keep getting stopped on my way to my car. I have three separate conversations. I can see Liam waiting by the door. I try to hurry. I don't want him to leave, because these other guys I'm talking to are definitely not my future husband. I'm still not going to say hi to Liam, but when I pass him, he says, "Hey, are you on the tennis team?"

"Yeah! You play football, right?"

It's all very casual, but inside I'm squealing. We end up talking with Tara for a while. The three of us decide to go to 7-Eleven, then to Liam's apartment. We hang out in the backyard. I'm silently freaking out the whole time. Everything with Arik is so complicated. Liam is hot and straitlaced, but I assume he has some kind of complicated past, because I've heard he's waiting to go on mission, which means he screwed around. I love that he's not too innocent. Now that I have a rocky past, I know I can't ever be with someone who isn't experienced. I wouldn't want to feel judged. And I wouldn't want to be with someone who doesn't know what they are doing sexually.

I get Liam's number that night. We hang out a few times, usually in a group, because even though things are rocky with Arik, I love him and don't want to physically cheat.

Still, I'm getting frustrated by our relationship. Arik's baby is due in a few months, but we never talk about it. I don't even know for sure if it's his. And the distance is hard. I'm exhausted after tennis practice and don't want to drive to West Jordan all the time, and there have been multiple nights where he was supposed to come to my place but bailed.

One night, I make him a full-on dinner and he never shows up. I'm standing in my kitchen in front of a heaping bowl of pesto pasta. I've bought his favorite drink: blue Powerade. I call him, and text him, and wait, then end up eating a huge portion of pasta and putting the rest in the fridge for leftovers.

The next morning, he texts me to say that he fell asleep. In my gut, I don't entirely believe him. But I don't want to be the kind of girl to freak out and pick a fight.

LIAM WANTS TO PLAY tennis with me. He thinks he can beat me, which is the pickup line every guy has used on me since I got to BYU.

I have no interest in spending another second playing tennis. I'm playing four hours a day and taking steroids for an overuse injury in my labrum, but I meet Liam and Tara at the BYU courts anyway. It's fun to play together, actually—entirely different from playing with my mom and Dick in California. The three of us have fun. I can't handle how hot Liam is.

He's goofy too. He makes me laugh. He's even sillier than Arik, and kind of wholesome too. He has ten siblings and grew up on a farm feeding chickens at five a.m.

Afterward, I have to run because Arik has a preseason scrimmage: SLCC is playing BYU. I literally race over to the fields to watch him pitch. I like having more than one guy: it makes me feel powerful. And it's a protective mechanism too. But when Arik points up at me from the dugout and shows me off to his teammates, I feel bad, like I've done something wrong.

MAYCI NEELEY

IT'S HALLOWEEN AND I'M at a party at Nicole's town house. I'm wearing a sexy CEO costume I bought on Main Street. It's a black leather miniskirt I've paired with red stripper heels, a lace bralette, and a cropped white button-down. I'm waiting for Arik to text me. He's at a baseball team bonding activity and we're supposed to meet up afterward. He texts to say he's having people over to his apartment. I ask him when I should come, then fill a Styrofoam Swig cup with someone else's alcohol and wait to hear back from him.

After an hour, I text him, "Am I good to come now?" He doesn't respond. I double text. I say, "Hey? Are you home?"

No response. I'm not going to drive to West Jordan if Arik is screwing around somewhere else. I wait a little longer, then text Liam, who's been asking to hang out.

I don't invite him to the party, because people are drinking, and I don't want him to get that impression of me. But I ask if he wants to get together.

He says yes, and at eleven, we meet at my apartment. It's cold, and we go inside. I can tell Liam doesn't feel comfortable going into my room. He stands at the bedroom door, looking inside but not going in. I don't push it.

We go to the couch and watch a movie on my laptop. We're cuddling, but I know I can't kiss him. I'm OK emotionally cheating, but actually kissing is crossing a line.

When he turns his face toward mine, I offer him my cheek. At five a.m., when he finally gets up to leave, he tries to kiss me again, and I dodge his face.

Once he's gone, I reach for my phone. Arik's texted saying that he left his phone in someone's car. He invites me to come sleep over at his place now.

I read his message twice, annoyed, then write a long text breaking up with him. I tell him I love him but it's over.

I'm too much of a pansy to end our relationship in person. But I know I'm done.

I assume Arik isn't going to care. He's been so MIA recently. But in the morning, Arik sends me a long text. He loves me. He really wants to give this a shot. He's attached a YouTube link to a song called "Please Forgive Me."

It's one of the songs we always listen to together. Selfishly, it warms my heart that he's fighting for me and is worried that he might lose me.

I still want to try things out with Liam, but I tell Arik we can talk in person. It's a Sunday, and I'm supposed to go to Lauren's house for dinner, like I do almost every week. It's something I look forward to. I have a game plan: I decide to invite Liam. If he can come, I'll try to make things work with him. If he can't, I'll at least hear Arik out.

Liam's busy, so I go to my sister's house, and then meet up with Arik. When I get to his apartment, he's quiet. We both are. Neither of us talks about the fact that I broke up with him over text less than twenty-four hours ago. Instead, we drive to Taco Bell. By the time we've gone through the drive-through, we're cracking jokes. We eat in the car, then go back to his apartment and have sober sex. The more comfortable I get with him, the more I'm able to have sex without being blackout drunk. I don't even feel that guilty for sleeping with him anymore. Every once in a while, the Mormon values will hit me, and I'll feel like a slut and wonder who will want to marry me at this point if things don't work out with Arik. But mostly, with Arik, I don't even care.

Lying in bed afterward, it feels like the breakup never even happened.

TWENTY-TWO

I TELL ARIK THE WORST THING THAT COULD HAPPEN TO ME is getting pregnant. We're at his apartment. He tells me I'm being paranoid. "Mayci," he says, "it's fine," and then we drive to get a blue Nerds Slush from Sonic. By the time we're in the car together, laughing about something totally unrelated, I'm not worried anymore. It's always like that with Arik. I feel fearless with him. Carefree. But when I'm alone in my apartment and he's thirty-five minutes away at his place in West Jordan, the doubts creep in. I tell myself that it's good I'm worried about getting pregnant because it means I'm paying attention. Naïve people get pregnant, not people who are aware of the risks. But I'm still anxious.

I'm not on birth control. It's too hard to get. I'd have to go through BYU Athletics, and then they'd know I was having sex and breaking the honor code. I can't go to a gynecologist in California, because then my parents would know. I think about going to the Planned Parenthood in Salt Lake, but it closes at four, which is when I'm at tennis practice.

Arik and I use condoms most of the time, but if we're drinking, we forget. He tries to pull out, but the pull-out method isn't perfect, and I end up taking Plan B a lot. I take it so often that fall that my face is constantly broken out and my period is completely out of whack. But I know something can still happen. I'm relieved every time I get my period. It's like, *Thank goodness. Everything is all right.*

IN NOVEMBER, ARIK'S PARENTS say they want to take us to dinner. Both of us freak out. We know it means they want to talk to us about something serious.

Arik says, "They definitely know something."

We're sitting on his bed.

"Like what?"

"I don't know," he says.

I don't want to go to the dinner. I like Arik's parents, and I know they like me too. But I tell Arik, "These are your parents. Why do I have to go again?"

Arik says he doesn't want to talk to them alone. We're laughing as we speculate about what we'll talk about at dinner; we're both clearly anxious. Arik keeps playing with his hat.

DINNER IS AT A pho place in Provo. It's nice. Fun, even. Afterward, we go to Arik's parents' condo in the Wells Fargo Building across the street. There's a kitchen on the left and a little family room. I'm so nervous that I say I need the bathroom, just to have a moment to hide. I walk back through the hall, lock the door, and stare at myself in the mirror. My eyeliner is too heavy, and my hair is parted on the side. I take a couple steadying breaths, flush the toilet even though I didn't use it, then wash my hands and go back out to the living room.

Arik's dad Jeff is sitting in a chair in the corner. His mom Liz is on the floor beside him. I sit next to Arik on the couch. I'm sure I have pit stains at this point because I can't stop sweating.

Arik's dad leans forward and says, "We know you guys are screwing around. We know you're drinking and having sex."

He's not angry, and neither is Arik's mom. But they are disappointed. They emphasize that Arik and I are both athletes. They don't want us to jeopardize our athletic careers.

"What's important right now is baseball," Arik's dad says. He turns to me. "And Mayci, your tennis career." He stares between us. "You don't want to let all that go because of a little screwing around, do you?"

I've never had someone sit me down and calmly lecture me like this. It's not my parents' style. They would probably kick my ass if they knew what I was doing. And nobody in my family even knows I'm dating Arik. They don't know anything about my life: nothing about drinking, or partying, or smoking weed. If they had even an inkling of what I've been up to since leaving Coto de Caza, they'd drag me home in a heartbeat.

"This is a new era for me," I tell Jeff and Liz. "I'm usually good." I force myself to look them in the eye. "I'm not a partier. I'm not someone who has sex with people. I'm not this wild girl or anything like that. All of this is very unlike me."

Arik's parents listen to me. I truly hope they believe me because I'm telling them the truth. They tell me that they like me, that they appreciate that Arik and I have talked about marriage, and that they're supportive of the fact that both of us want to get married in the temple one day.

"That's my goal," I tell them. "It'll always be my goal."

"Then you guys have to stop this behavior," Jeff says. "Turn this around—"

"We're not telling you to break up," Liz interjects. "We know you guys love each other and we love you together." I can tell that they genuinely support us as a couple. "We just want you to make better decisions, OK?"

I leave the condo feeling glad the conversation happened. I know I haven't been making good choices. Despite having barely gone to church, I have always known I want to come back to church and be a good Mormon again. Long-term, I want to have a family and get married in the temple. Partying and having sex out of wedlock is a phase. It's time to be better and turn my life back around.

But I don't know how to stop. Arik and I are having too much fun together. And once you've had sex with someone and you love them, it's almost impossible to just not. We try. We both think his parents are right. We have a long conversation about it at my apartment later that night, where we agree we need to try harder.

That lasts all of two days.

We can't keep our hands off each other. Now that we're having sex when I'm sober, it's all I want to do. People might say it's because of Arik. But it's definitely me too.

TWENTY-THREE

ARIK'S PARENTS HAVE A HOUSE IN SAINT GEORGE. WE decide to go for the weekend. While we're out there, I give him his dog tag back. Neither of us is mushy, but it's an important moment. Arik posts it on Snapchat with the caption "This guy is lucky."

My parents call when we're in Saint George. They ask what I'm doing. I say I'm on a hike with my roommates. Arik's parents call, and he lies too.

It's a thrill to dodge the adults in our lives.

We take pictures of his parents' house so we can put everything back where we found it. Arik's mom never pushes the kitchen stools all the way in, so Arik tells me to leave them out. We get In-N-Out for dinner to avoid messing up the kitchen. We tiptoe on the rug to leave no footprints, and we're crazy careful with the beds, since Arik tells me they have a display of twenty pillows that are in a certain order.

We drink Mike's Hard Lemonades in the Jacuzzi, then have sex in Arik's parents' shower. Arik hasn't turned on the water heater properly, so it's ice-cold, but we don't care. In the morning, we take his family's Mini Cooper out and drive too fast. In the passenger seat, my hands out the window, I feel completely free. I'm invincible. Nothing can touch me.

Later, Arik and I drive a scooter on the golf course to watch the sunset. I feel like I'm thirteen again. Arik and I don't stop laughing all weekend. We're in love, and we're young, and everything is perfect. We don't mention the conversation with his parents, or the fact that Arik's ex-girlfriend is eight months pregnant, or that I completely ghosted Liam.

I NEVER THINK ABOUT how hard all of this is for Arik. I don't think about how painful and confusing it must be to have to leave school, to have an ex who's about to give birth, to be sleeping with someone new. It's too much for me to even imagine, and I'm scared to bring it up.

Looking back, I can see it was probably eating him alive. But at nineteen, I was oblivious. I just tried not to think about it. And that breaks my heart. I wish I'd been mature enough to face it head-on.

TWENTY-FOUR

ARIK'S BABY IS BORN. I DON'T SPEND A LOT OF TIME THINKing about what it means for him to be a parent, or what it means for his ex-girlfriend to be raising a kid alone. After Dick, the last thing I want is another chaotic, messy relationship. I want to have fun.

And we do. For Christmas, Arik comes over to my apartment with a stack of presents. He gives me an Abercrombie jacket, a bracelet, and hoop earrings. It's clear he went shopping with his mom at the mall. I give him a Brixton Snapback hat and Nike SB sneakers, but he says all he really wants is a letter telling him how I feel. That's my worst nightmare. I'm not a sentimental person. But I try to write something meaningful for him, and a couple days later, I take the letter to his apartment. He doesn't just want me to hand it to him. He wants me to read it aloud. I sit next to him on his bed and tell him that being with him is the best adventure of my life. I tell him how free he makes me. How with him, I'm spontaneous. How he makes me want to experience things I never have before.

I tell him that I know the circumstances we're fighting aren't ideal, but that we've saved each other, that I miss him the second we say goodbye, that I can imagine a future with him. I write that no matter what happens, I'll always love him. I end the letter with "One Day," which is a phrase we always tell each other; something we both have written in our Instagram bios. And I call him Albert, because when he doesn't wear a hat, his wild hair makes him look like Einstein.

Arik cries when I read him the letter, and I do too.

MAYCI NEELEY

I MISS ARIK OVER Christmas break, and I beg my dad to fly me back to Utah for New Year's. My mom is like, "Absolutely not." But I tell my dad I want to go out with some girlfriends. He's a big friend guy—he wants me to have a solid community of friends. My mom Cindy is like, "Marshall, what are you doing? Don't let her go." But my lie works.

Arik takes me to a concert at the Great Saltair. There are multiple DJs playing to ring in 2015. We have friends buy us alcohol, and we drink it in Arik's car in the parking lot before the show. I'm used to taking Dick's prescription pills when I party. Arik has an Oxy prescription for his shoulder injury. I take one and wash it down with a shot. I figure it's a special occasion. We're hammered by the time we should be getting out of the car and going into the concert. Instead, we stay in the car and hang out. We don't talk about anything deep—like how he hasn't met his baby yet because his lawyer advised him not to until they're certain it's his kid. I don't know if Arik is even in touch with his ex at this point, or if she's sent him a picture of the baby. It's all out of sight, out of mind. When I'm sober, I sometimes get stuck on it. But when I'm drunk and high, it's like it doesn't even exist.

After an hour, we go into the concert, where we meet one of his cousins. Dick has texted me, so I'm paranoid that he's at the concert and is going to hurt me. But once Arik and I are dancing, I have fun. I'm completely wasted.

In all of my photos and videos of that night, my arms are around Arik's neck, my black top falling down, my body pressed against his.

At midnight, we take a video of me kissing him. I'm wearing his dog tag.

FIND MY FRIENDS ISN'T really a thing yet, so I don't worry about my parents realizing how much time I spend at Arik's apartment in West Jordan. I only have to think about them when they're in Utah. Unfortunately, that's literally all the time. My mom is constantly with us because of Lauren's maternity arrangement with BYU Athletics. And on January 3, my whole family comes to town for a cousin's wedding.

I feel bloated that morning. When I see my lower stomach in the mirror, I think, OK, that's not good. It doesn't feel any better when I get to Lauren's house and everyone is like, "Mayci, you look horrible." My eyeliner looks like I slept in it, and I'm wearing a sort of messy side ponytail that isn't doing me any favors. Lauren changes my hair, and we all drive to the wedding in Salt Lake City. I spend a lot of the day holding Presley, who's wearing a black sweater over her tulle dress.

MY MOM'S BIRTHDAY IS the next day. I'm still feeling off. Right before family dinner, I scroll Instagram and see a picture of a random account showcasing a pregnancy test. The caption reads, "It's not the end of the world. It's the start of new life." I take a screenshot, then try to forget about it.

A week later, Arik and I get drunk and spend a night at the Little America Hotel. It's a mini staycation in Salt Lake City. I wear the Abercrombie jacket he got me for Christmas. We go to the Clark Planetarium. Arik loves space.

We walk through the carpeted building, kissing beneath the replicas of the planets that hang overhead. Jupiter, Neptune, Saturn.

I sleep at Arik's place that night. We have sex. I'm on top of him when I feel like things are different from usual.

I stop moving and ask him, "Does this feel weird?"

He pulls out. We both look down and see blood everywhere.

His bedspread—gray and white with vertical navy stripes—looks like a crime scene. I think it's the beginning of my period. I go to the bathroom, where I start feeling sick: a combination of horrible cramps and nausea. It doesn't feel normal, but I don't know what to do, so I ask Arik to go out to the car and get a tampon for me.

I put it in, and then we curl up on the couch and watch a movie together. During the movie I feel so ill that I want to puke, but I fall asleep instead.

In the morning, I take out the tampon and it's completely dry. No blood. Nothing.

I'm like, *What the hell is happening with my body?*

I feel better, but I'm confused and still a little sick. I don't know anything about pregnancy, but obviously I'm worried. Could I have miscarried? Could it have been a short period? Could it be from all the morning-after pills I've taken this year?

It doesn't even occur to me to go to the doctor or the ER. I'm more like, *Whoops, sorry about your bedspread, Arik, hope that stain comes out in the wash!* And a part of me is hoping that if I *was* pregnant, all that blood was a miscarriage. I don't say that to anyone, because I still think I'm being paranoid. But a small voice in my head knows I'm pregnant. Or knows I was.

TWENTY-FIVE

I FIND LETTERS TUCKED ON THE SIDE OF ARIK'S DRESSER. They're from professional baseball teams. I turn to him and ask, "Are you going to open those?"

I'm staring at the Washington Nationals logo: a curling *W*.

Arik doesn't answer me. I don't know why he's not excited about this. Maybe he's distracted by everything that's going on. But he has an incredible future ahead of him. I want him to be able to see that. I want him to take a breath, to confide in me, to open the envelopes. But he doesn't. I never see him tear into a single one.

I don't push him, because I'm in my own head too. I'm pretty sure I could still be pregnant. It's tennis season, and I'm in great shape. I'm playing four hours a day. But I feel winded walking to class or up the stairs. And my lower stomach is still bloated.

On January 21, I'm supposed to fly to California for my brother's wedding. The night before, I cry to Arik about my period. I'm convinced it's not going to come.

Arik tells me I'm being paranoid and that I don't need to worry. I try to believe him, but I just have this feeling in my gut.

I'm anxious all weekend. After the rehearsal dinner, when McCall and I have walked out to the parking lot together, she tells me she's pregnant. It's almost a relief to hear it. If I'm pregnant, too, I won't have to go through it all alone.

I ask her what her symptoms are, mostly to see if I'm experiencing the same ones. She says her boobs are really sore, especially at her armpits. Mine are too.

I say, "Oh, that's so interesting! What else?"

She names other symptoms. I have them all.

Every time she says one aloud, I say, "Wow! OK!"

The next day is the wedding. My period isn't late, yet, but I feel different. Off. I try to pretend everything's fine. I wear a red lip and the gold sequined skirt my brother's wife picked out for the bridal party. When a friend offers me a shot of vodka, I feel too worried about a potential pregnancy to take it.

BACK IN PROVO, I lose my season opener against Utah State. My parents are there, watching. I can tell they're worried. It should've been an easy win. But my arms feel like they're made out of cooked spaghetti. I literally can't breathe each time I run for the ball. And my labrum, which I've been taking steroids for, hurts. The pain goes down my arm and into my fingertips. I feel like I have the flu.

After the match, I can't even move my wrist, because my whole right arm is so swollen. The loss is an ego crush: for me and the team. Lauren is mad. I'm confused. I'm like, *Why do I feel this way? Am I pregnant? Is my life over?*

THE NEXT DAY, NICOLE gets baptized. Arik and his parents come to the church, along with my whole family. Some of us go out to dinner afterward at Los Hermanos in Provo: tan stars hang from the ceiling. There's a tiled fish on one of the walls. I invite Arik to tag along. I tell my parents he's a friend. If I am pregnant, I want to incorporate him more into my life. But my dad completely ignores him. He's seen Snapchats from Arik, whose profile name is ArikMackDaddy69, so he's opposed to him on principle.

Nicole is planning on getting engaged soon, so we all look at rings. Lauren notices Arik and me talking about his mom's ring and is like, *Why are Mayci and Arik talking about engagement rings?* Nobody in my family even thinks we're dating.

LAUREN HAS A SUPER Bowl party. I invite Arik. I say he's only a friend, again, but I can tell she notices that it's the second time in five days that I've brought him to something.

That week, she talks to a member of the BYU coaching staff about Arik. He tells Lauren that Arik got a girl pregnant the year before. He says that Arik is a nice guy, that there's no bad blood, but that I should probably avoid him. Lauren tells my parents, which puts them on edge. I get why they're worried, but it's ironic: years later, this same member of the coaching staff will be caught having an affair with the mom of one of his recruits, so I'm not totally sure about his judgment.

THERE'S MORE TENNIS TO play. I fly to Denver with the team. I beat Maureen Slattery at the Denver Country Club in the first set 6–1, and 7–5 in the second. I can't catch my breath. Later, Lauren tells me that's when she knew I was pregnant, or at least suspected it. She watched me huffing and puffing on the court and felt sure something was off. At the time, though, when she asks me what's wrong after the match, I tell her it's my asthma. She goes to the trainers and talks to them. They discuss getting me in to see a doctor or finding me a new inhaler. I want to believe that'll solve everything, but when I get to my hotel that night, I can't stop obsessing over my stomach. I pull up my BYU T-shirt and take a selfie, my phone plugged into the outlet on the side of the bed. I'm sharing a room with my teammate Amy. She takes a Snapchat of me taking a photo of my stomach.

That night, Arik's acting off. He's not answering my texts, and when he does later, he sounds different. We have a rule not to drink when we're not together. We both know it makes us act out. I get the feeling he's drinking. I can't be that mad. I've broken that rule too. But I'm annoyed at him anyway.

And a small part of me worries about cheating. I know I've emotionally cheated on him with Liam, but I wonder if there's a possibility he's *actually* cheating on me. He's too mushy when he finally responds, so I know something is off. He says he loves me over and over. He calls me baby. He's acting like someone else. We never talk to each other like that over text. I text him back, "You're being sketch," and then I go to sleep.

TWENTY-SIX

I NEED TO BUY A PREGNANCY TEST. I TELL MYSELF IT'S FOR peace of mind. I'm not pregnant. I just need to make sure everything is OK. But I don't quite believe it.

I ask Nicole to take me to a CVS. It's the same one I went to with Dick the year before, when he threw the Plan B across the front seat at me. I feel self-conscious in the store, like everyone is looking at me. I don't hear anything Nicole says. I'm in my own world. I get the test—the kind with two lines—and then we go to Del Taco, where I buy Nicole lunch to thank her for coming.

She drops me off outside my apartment. I get out of her car, the CVS bag tucked in my jacket pocket. Before I'm inside, she's driven off to hang out with her boyfriend.

I read the instructions alone in my apartment bathroom, my hands shaking. I decide I want to pee in a cup because I've never peed on a stick before and I truly don't know how that's supposed to work. I go into the kitchen and get a red Solo cup. Then I pee, plop the test in the cup on the counter, take it out, and go lie in bed. I have a feeling the test is going to be positive. But I'm also in denial: I can't be pregnant. I so badly don't want to be pregnant. Shouldn't I be able to will the test to be negative?

My mattress is creaky and uncomfortable. I lie on it for twenty minutes, the sun setting outside. I've taped turquoise sheets across the window to block the light, so the whole room looks almost blue.

I don't look at my phone. I don't do anything. I have too much anxiety. Eventually, when I know I can't put it off anymore, I go and look at the test.

At first, I think it's negative. I only see one dark line. But when I shine my phone's flashlight, I can see another faint one. I feel like I'm going to throw up. I grab my laptop, the Mac I've had since I was thirteen, place it on the toilet lid, and sit in the shower sobbing to the saddest songs I can find. I stay in there until it's pitch-black outside and the only light is the glow from my computer screen. I think my life is completely over.

When I get out of the shower, I pray for the first time in more than a year. I feel like I can't tell anyone about the results of the test, so I talk to God.

I say, "*Please help me, please help me, please help me.*"

IN THE MORNING, I feel a little better. Maybe I read the test wrong. I stick it in a textbook and bring it to the Student Athlete Building, where, over lunch at Legends Grille, I show Tara. The line is so faint. But we both think I'm pregnant. I feel like I am. And my boobs have gotten really big. Even Lauren notices when I wear a tight pink shirt to practice. My skin is awful, too, which doesn't help my confidence. I have small bumps from my mouth to my ears on both sides of my face. It makes me look like the Joker from *The Dark Knight*. And it convinces me that if I am pregnant, I'm having a girl, because everyone says girls steal your beauty.

I TAKE ANOTHER TEST a week later. The pack I had contained two, and I need to know for sure. I've been in a state of denial. When this one is positive, I feel resigned and defeated. I stare at the second line and think, *Mayci, you dumbass, you're knocked-up, your life is over.* Then I pray again.

I need to talk to Arik. I drive the thirty-five minutes to West Jordan. I've done the drive so many times I don't even see the road anymore. When I get off the highway at his exit, I'm panicking. I call him and he comes out to get me, then takes me through his trashed kitchen and into his room. We get in bed and watch *Lord of the Rings* on his laptop. I don't actually watch any of it. I lie beside him and, through sobs, tell him I'm pregnant. I don't break up with him exactly, but I'm trying to pick a fight. I say all the reasons this won't work. He hasn't gone on mission. My parents are going to hate that his ex-girlfriend has a baby. He had to leave BYU. His Snapchat name is my dad's worst nightmare. My voice is scratchy and I'm talking too fast.

But Arik is calm. He reminds me that we've already talked about getting married. Neither of us thought it was going to happen anytime soon, but we both want it. This doesn't make me feel better. We both want to be professional athletes too. I want to go on a humanitarian trip to Morocco or do an internship in London. Arik has dreams of his own. Neither of us is in a rush to get married, let alone have a baby.

Arik holds me and says, "This is just changing the plan a little bit." He tells me everything is going to work out.

FOR THREE WEEKS, ARIK and I hold our secret. It feels like we're in our own little world. We talk about the baby: how we think she'll have blue eyes and how we're both positive she's a girl. We decide we're going to name her Marley Mack because I love Bob Marley and I like the idea of an M name. One day, when we're in the shower together, Arik writes "Marley Mack" in the steam on the glass wall.

When I'm with Arik, I feel OK about the baby. But the second I'm alone again, I panic. I think about miscarrying; how it would be a relief if I lost the baby. I feel guilty for thinking this, but each time I play a match or go to lift weights, I wonder if squatting or serving will knock something out of place. I go on extra runs and work out hard. Maybe I can make myself miscarry. As disgusting as this sounds, I secretly hope I do.

A lot of the girls on the tennis team know about the baby, but they don't tell Lauren. When she asks them what's going on with me, they say they don't know.

One afternoon, at practice, Lauren notices how tired I look. She asks Demi, who's on the team and in my year, what she knows.

MAYCI NEELEY

"Mayci is acting so weird," Lauren says. "She better not be pregnant."

Demi lies to Lauren for me, but I know I'm going to have to tell my family at some point. I want to wait until I'm through the first trimester. So many people have miscarriages. Maybe I'll lose the baby and not have to tell anyone. Maybe I'll step in front of a car and die.

TWENTY-SEVEN

ON MY TWENTIETH BIRTHDAY, TENNIS PRACTICE ENDS early. There's no weight training. I ask my friend Amy to come with me to the Pregnancy Resource Center. It's next to Planned Parenthood. Usually, both clinics are closed by the time I'm free. Abortion doesn't even occur to me as an option. And I don't know that Planned Parenthood offers ultrasounds. I assume it's just for abortions and birth control.

The Pregnancy Resource Center will see me without taking insurance, meaning nobody will find out I'm going. When Amy and I get there, two women take us to a back room. We sit. I tell them I'm pregnant. They have me take a pee test and wait for the results. I know it'll be positive, but it's still shocking to hear someone say the words out loud. One of the women—I think she's a counselor—immediately asks me how the positive pregnancy test makes me feel.

"Well, not good," I say, trying to hold back tears.

The Pregnancy Resource Center is a Christian organization. They have a statement of faith on their website. It's clear they don't want me to get an abortion. And I don't want to get one either. I've grown up pro-life. I've always thought women should be able to get abortions for rape or incest, but this baby feels like a consequence of my own actions. I chose to have sex and I knew the outcome could be a baby. It's my responsibility to bear it.

These days, I feel differently. I survived my teen pregnancy because I had resources. I survived because I wasn't in an abusive relationship, because my family could help me, because my baby wasn't endangering my life. But so many people aren't in that position. Over the years, I've become more of a feminist. I believe it's not up to me to judge what other women do. Abortion isn't the problem. The problem is the lack of resources for women. I should've been able to get birth control in college easily without having to drive an hour to Planned Parenthood and without seeing an OB-GYN. And, *hello*, shouldn't we have birth control for men by now? The responsibility should not solely fall on women. I should've learned basic sex ed instead of taking BYU's class on marriage and family twice for easy credits.

I feel similarly about drinking. I carry so much shame about the times I drank and drove. When I teach my kids about alcohol, I'll tell them I hope they choose not to drink. But I'll also tell them that if they do, they need to not drive.

Nobody ever explained that to me. It was all about abstinence. The reality is, kids will drink, and have sex, and make mistakes—it's better to give them information than set a hard line that not everyone will follow. My sisters followed that hard line to a T, but my personality has always been more curious. And statistically speaking, if you have more than one kid, chances are, you're going to get at least one who doesn't follow the guidelines religiously.

IN THE CLINIC, THE women show me the size of my baby using a model. We talk a little while longer, then go to a second room, where one of the women—the tech, wearing pink scrubs, her brown hair down—does an ultrasound on my belly.

The baby looks like a ball of mush. I see almost nothing at all.

She tells me she wants to do a vaginal ultrasound so we can get more information. I'm embarrassed to lie back on the plastic sheet on the table and spread my legs. I've never done any of this before. I've never even been to a gynecologist.

During the vaginal ultrasound, I can see little fingers, arms, legs, eyes. I understand, for the first time, that I'm carrying a baby. There's no hematoma on the ultrasound. It could've healed in the three weeks since I bled on Arik's sheets, but it's unlikely.

The tech says that because I've been taking steroids for my labrum, the baby could have a cleft lip. She tells me we won't know until my twenty-week ultrasound, and that based on the baby's measurements, I'm almost ten weeks along. I haven't been planning on telling anyone about my pregnancy until I'm out of the first trimester, in case I miscarry and get in trouble for nothing. But it seems like this baby is staying put. And for the first time, it feels real. For the first time, I feel content that I am going to be a mom. For the first time, I feel attached and protective of this little life growing inside of me.

A COUPLE DAYS LATER, my mom calls while I'm getting out of the elevator in my apartment. She wants to know what I did for my birthday. I tell her Arik took me out to dinner at La Jolla Groves. I know my parents don't approve of him, but I'm ten weeks pregnant with his baby. There's nothing to hide anymore.

Later, when I'm driving to Arik's apartment, my dad calls and starts yelling.

"You need to break up with him!" he shouts.

I'm going sixty miles an hour. I pull over, my heart racing. My dad says if I don't end things with Arik, he's going to step in and handle it.

"Dad—" I say.

"No," he interrupts. "You break up with him tonight, or I'll call his parents."

I can't imagine my dad talking to Liz and Jeff, not when they know we're drinking and having sex and my parents don't.

I grip the steering wheel and say, "OK."

"Do it," he says.

TWENTY-EIGHT

NICOLE AND I ARE SITTING IN MY CAR OUTSIDE MY SISter's house. I don't know why I've brought her with me, except I don't want to talk to Lauren about my pregnancy alone. Telling her makes the consequences real. It means I've failed both of us.

Inside, Nicole, Lauren, and I talk about Lauren's new couch. We're in the family room. Lauren is facing the kitchen. Nicole and I are opposite her, looking at the back wall. The conversation is awkward. Nicole is staring at Lauren, who's clearly waiting for me to explain why we've driven twenty minutes to her house. I can tell Lauren wants to know why I've brought Nicole too. Later, she'll tell me she thought, *Why the heck is she here? This is a personal family thing.*

The new couch is made of some gray woven material that doesn't stain. I can't focus on the conversation. Twenty miles away, Arik is telling his family that I'm pregnant. I imagine him sitting his parents down. I picture them in their living room and wonder if his dad will still like me.

"So," Lauren says, staring at me. "Is anything new?"

I start crying. Beside me, I feel Nicole stiffen.

"I didn't get my period," I say.

Lauren asks if I took a test.

"Yeah." I wipe my cheeks. "It was positive."

Lauren asks Nicole to call her boyfriend to come pick her up. She's completely calm. She says she needs to talk to me one-on-one.

When Nicole leaves, Lauren turns to me and says I need to tell our parents. Now. I ask her if we can just hide the pregnancy until the semester ends. But Lauren says I have to tell them. I've signed the BYU honor code, which I've basically walked all over. I've lied, I've drunk, I've smoked. I could probably cover all of that up, but my pregnancy blatantly violates the third item: "Live a chaste and virtuous life, including abstaining from sexual relations outside marriage." And Nicole has seen me tell my sister, meaning if anyone else finds out, BYU will know she helped me hide my pregnancy. That would put Lauren at risk of losing her job.

"Do it," Lauren says, and I fish out my phone.

"Can't we wait?" I ask. "We can tell them when they're here in a couple weeks." I look at her, pleading. "In person is better."

"No," Lauren says. "We're doing it now." She says I can't dump this on her and expect her not to say anything.

I call my dad first. He's more logical about issues like this and less likely to shout at me. He's on a business trip to Modesto, and the first thing he asks when he answers is "Did you break up with him?" He sounds happy, as if he's expecting me to tell him I took his advice. I start crying. My dad's voice changes. "Are you pregnant?" he asks.

"Yes."

He doesn't yell at me, but I can tell he's pissed. He warned me about Arik. And he tried to help me with Dick. He says we need to call my mom.

"No," I say. "Can you just tell her?"

I desperately don't want to talk to my mom about this, but my dad says I need to break the news. He hangs up and I call her myself. She's in a good mood when she answers, but she's a little confused. She wants to know why I'm calling so late. When I tell her I'm pregnant, she's furious. I've only ever heard her say the F word twice in my life until today, but she uses it and calls me a slut. I know what I've done, so hearing her call me a slut doesn't hurt me. I'm like, *Yes, I know, that's how we got here, can we move on to what we're going to do next?*

Then my mom gets mad at my dad. She's convinced I got pregnant on New Year's. It becomes a point of contention for my parents. My mom thinks if my dad hadn't flown me back for the concert with Arik, none of this would've happened. She makes it seem like my pregnancy is my dad's fault because he let me go.

I tell my mom I was already pregnant by then. Based on my due date, I must've gotten pregnant in December, which also explains why I was already feeling weird at my cousin's wedding. But my mom is still angry.

My dad calls back. He says he's flying to Utah the next day. He's bringing me home. He tells me I can't see Arik again, then hangs up so he can book his flight.

I look at Lauren, who stands, hugs me, and starts to cry. She says being a mom is the hardest thing she's ever done. I pull back, feeling scared.

Kirk has been putting Presley to bed. He comes downstairs, sees Lauren and me both crying on the new gray couch, and asks, "What's up?"

Between sobs, Lauren tells him, "You're going to be an uncle."

"What?"

"Mayci's pregnant."

Kirk is calm. I can tell he's trying to wrap his mind around all of this. He asks me a few questions, then says, "Well, shit. OK!" I can tell Lauren is glad he's talking to me, because it gives her a second to come up with a game plan.

She says we need to go talk to the athletic director and the dean of students the next day. She'll give them a heads-up that we're coming. She'll be at my apartment at eight a.m. She and my dad are both planners: in a crisis, they want a series of tasks they can execute.

I tell Lauren and Kirk I need to go home. Lauren is a rule-follower, so she stands and reminds me not to see Arik. I tell her, "No problem," then I text him and ask him to meet me at my apartment.

I'm relieved when I see him. We get in my bed, where he tells me how supportive his parents were; how they think we should move in with them; how they're willing to help us financially with the baby. Don't get me wrong, they're not *happy* we ignored their advice. Arik tells me his mom cried when he told her and that he hated to see her upset. But overall, they're understanding. Their reaction is so different from my parents', who never want me to talk to Arik again.

I tell Arik I can't move in with him. I love him, I want to be with him, but I have to go home. My parents are my support system. I can't just give everything up and stay in Utah. Even my Audi—the one thing I kind of own—is in my dad's name until I graduate. If I turn my back on my family, I'll have nothing.

Arik is frantic. He says I need to stay. We can get married. We can be together.

"I have to leave," I tell him, my eyes streaming. "I don't have another choice."

"You do," Arik says. "I'm offering you one."

I want to trust myself enough to stay. But all I've ever expected in my life is to be a tennis player or a stay-at-home mom. Both options are gone now that I'm pregnant. Nobody will want to marry me now that I'm not a virgin. My tennis career is ruined. I have no job skills and a tattered reputation. The only thing I have going for me is that my GPA has gone up. I've got a 2.4 now, thank you very much. I know I need my parents.

"I have to go," I tell Arik.

TWENTY-NINE

I FEEL SICK WHEN LAUREN PICKS ME UP AT MY APARTMENT the next morning. Arik and I stayed up all night talking, so I'm exhausted. My eyeballs ache. I'm nauseous. And I'm terrified of telling BYU about my pregnancy. I assume I'm going to get kicked out.

I can tell Lauren's on edge too. She's quiet on the short drive to the Student Athlete Building, where we meet with Tom, the athletic director.

He's been expecting us. We all make small talk, then do a quick prayer. Afterward, Lauren looks at me. I know I need to speak.

I turn to Tom and say, "I made a mistake." I'm crying. "I'm pregnant."

Tom stares at me across his desk and says, "A baby is never a mistake."

He's so much kinder than I expected. My eyes burn.

Tom goes on to tell me about other people who had babies and came back to BYU to play their sports. None of them had babies out of wedlock, but it makes me feel better anyway. I assumed this conversation would be terrible, but Tom makes me feel like a person, and like everything in my life might be OK. This conversation is one I'll never forget. He positively influenced me more than he'll ever know that day.

Tom and Lauren say they need to talk without me. The two of them leave me in his office and go down the hall, where Tom asks Lauren who the dad is. If it's a BYU student, he'll need to be held accountable. Lauren tells Tom that Arik has already left BYU.

When Tom and Lauren come back, he suggests that I withdraw from BYU so that I don't get in trouble for violating the honor code. That way, I can earn my ecclesiastical endorsement back while I'm pregnant and then return to school after I've given birth. Mormons usually have to repent for a year after having sex outside of marriage. I understand that my repenting can start now, meaning I should be able to be on campus for winter semester next year if I do everything right. This is a huge relief. It means I have a shot at playing tennis again, at earning a degree, at getting my life back.

"Thank you," I tell Tom through my tears.

LAUREN AND I TALK to Fui Vakapuna next. He's in charge of the honor code for athletics. I've always loved him. He was friends with Lauren in college, so he's been nice to me my entire time at BYU. He's chill and laid-back. He makes me feel more relaxed about having to leave BYU, which is good, because our last meeting of the day is with the dean of students, Vern Heperi.

I've never met him. Lauren and I drive over to the Wilkinson Student Center and park in the large lot out front. I feel numb and exhausted. We go up the stairs. Lauren doesn't look at me when I breathe heavily on the steps, but I know we both notice.

Inside, more stairs, these ones decorated with a painting of a cougar wearing a BYU football uniform. It's loud inside: I can hear students eating lunch, drinking caffeine-free Coke, studying, buying BYU merch from the campus store I haven't had to go to because I get so much free gear from tennis.

On the top floor, we turn left toward the dean's office. There's a wooden plaque enclosed in glass outside the office. It says CAMPUS LIFE in capital letters. I skim it. The deans want to help students feel engaged. They want to create community. They want to offer unique experiences.

I touch a hand to my belly and follow Lauren through the glass door.

We check in with the secretary, who sits behind a huge wooden table, then we sit in chairs in the waiting room.

I'm terrified to talk to Vern, but when he calls us back to his office, he's like a big teddy bear. He says, "Even if you don't come back here to play tennis, I want you to come back to BYU." It's so powerful for him to be that kind to me—for all three of my conversations to go so well. Tom, Fui, and Vern all make me feel less horrible about myself. They each make a real difference in my life by giving me choices and options I didn't think I'd have.

Before I leave Vern's office, he says, "We love you, Mayci. We want you to get yourself straight, have that baby, and come back to campus. When you get back here, I want to see you. I want to give you a hug."

LAUREN AND I GO back to my apartment, where we pack. I don't tell my roommates why I'm leaving, just that I'll be gone by that night.

Lauren takes the day off coaching so she can help me. She gets me enrolled in online school so I can come back to BYU and be NCAA eligible after having my baby. I'm not sure I'll want this yet, but it's good to have the option.

At my apartment, she tells me which of my clothes I should give away because I won't wear them once I'm a mom. No more red stripper heels. No more crop tops or short shorts. No more slutty CEO Halloween costume. (I probably should've kept it. It really helped me manifest my future as the CEO of Babymama.)

It's all depressing. We box up the clothes for Tara, then deep clean my room so I can get my deposit back. When I lift my mattress, I find a condom wrapper.

I throw it away immediately—so fast that Lauren doesn't see it—but the Mormon in me feels so ashamed. I know Lauren knows I've had sex. I'm literally pregnant. But I still feel humiliated. I've messed up so badly.

Afterward, we drive over to the indoor tennis courts so I can clean out my locker. I grab my rackets, my shoes, and my tennis bag. We're rushing because Lauren doesn't want us to run into the team. I take everything I need, and then we're out of there.

I GO BACK TO Lauren and Kirk's house that night. My dad has arrived. He wants to make sure I don't see Arik. I'm like, *What are you talking about? You think I'm not going to say bye to this man who's my boyfriend, whose baby I'm carrying?*

I tell my dad and Lauren that I need to drop off the clothes for Tara.

"Make sure you don't see Arik," my dad says. Lauren turns to Amy, who's at the house with us, and says, "Don't let her see him."

"I won't," Amy lies.

Everyone's acting like Arik is abusing me. I wish I could get them to understand how wrong they are. Dick abused me. Arik saved me. He's been the best thing to happen to me this year, not the worst.

Amy and I drive to a parking lot in Orem by an In-N-Out, where we meet Arik. I know it's going to be a short goodbye. We're not going to have a lot of time.

Amy parks. I get out of her car and walk over to Arik, who's sitting in his green Honda Element. We always called it the toaster. I open the driver's door and sit on his lap. He tells me he wants me to stay. He's frustrated and pleading, his voice cracking.

He says, "My parents will take care of everything." He's staying with them in Spanish Fork. "We won't have to worry about anything. Please, Mayci."

I'm tempted to stay in Utah with him—truly, that's all I want. But I know I can't disobey my parents. I can't make them even more upset than they already are. It's not who I am. I'm leaving Arik because I'm afraid of being more of a rebel. Because I need to figure out who I am and what I'm going to do with my life. I need a new plan.

Arik starts sobbing. "This is our life together," he says, his hands around my waist. I'm crying too. "This is our baby. How can you just leave and go to California?"

"I have to," I say.

We both say how much we love each other, and then I stand to leave. The whole conversation is short. A couple of minutes. Neither of us know this will be the last time we see each other in person.

THIRTY

My dad wants to drive from Utah to California in one day. "We've got ten hours," he says as we get on the freeway. "You might as well tell me everything."

"Everything?" I repeat.

"Yeah," he says.

I tell him about the abuse. I don't go into detail, because I don't want to be responsible for Dick's murder, but I give him the CliffsNotes. I say that I was assaulted. That Dick took my virginity. That he pressured me to drink and smoke. And I say that Arik is different.

"He makes me feel invincible," I say.

"Well, you're not," my dad says after a moment. "You're pregnant."

It's quiet in the Audi, and then I say, "I wish someone would punch me in the stomach. Then I could just go back to my life."

My dad nods, his eyes on the road, and asks if I've considered adoption. I haven't. Not really. Arik loves me and loves our baby. And I love him.

"Your mother and I support you, no matter what you choose," my dad says. "I just want to make sure you consider all your options and make the best decision for you."

I don't know what to say, so I start to talk about Arik. I want my dad to understand that Arik is different from Dick, but my dad interrupts me.

He says that Dick and Arik both took advantage of me. I try to explain that that's not true. Dick manipulated and abused me. Arik loves me and I love him. He and I messed up together.

My dad tells me I'm being naïve.

"Arik and I are talking about getting married," I tell him.

"No, you're not," he says.

IT'S LATE WHEN WE get to California. My family is grabbing Thai food. We meet them at the restaurant, where my mom gives me a hug and says, "There's my naughty daughter." She never leaves the house without her hair and makeup done. I'm in my ratty car clothes, and I smell like a gas station. Alex is happy to see me. But McCall is cold. She, Alex, and their spouses Katelyn and Alex D are living with my parents. It's going to be a full house.

In the car after dinner, my dad tells me that McCall's upset that I'm pregnant. "She planned her pregnancy," he tells me, navigating through Coto's two gates. "She did it the way you're supposed to. She wants her turn in the limelight."

"She can have it," I say.

I'm not frustrated by the idea of our family celebrating McCall's baby but not mine. McCall did everything right, while I've embarrassed myself and my whole family. I don't feel like I deserve anything right now—not even happiness.

WHEN I WAKE UP on my first day in California, it takes me a second to realize I'm in my childhood bedroom. I blink and sit up, texting Arik before I go downstairs. My family's made it clear they don't want me communicating with him, which I think is unfair. But it doesn't seem right to rub our texts and calls in their faces, either—not when they're housing and feeding me. I feel like a burden they have to deal with.

At breakfast, I try to have a good attitude. But I feel like I'm in high school again. And I'm hurt by how mean McCall is. I thought we'd be able to talk about our pregnancies together and bond. I thought we'd make our own little support group.

Instead, she tells me I should give my baby up for adoption. I know it's a jealousy thing. This is supposed to be her moment: her turn to have a baby, her turn to be the center of attention. It's hard to be the middle child. But it's not like I asked for any of this. Does she think I want to be a pregnant twenty-year-old studying for a finance class in my parents' house? Does she think I want my days to consist of homework, self-loathing, and eating takeout with my family when I should be finishing my sophomore year of tennis? Does she think I want to have a baby by myself instead of going to school?

I complain about McCall to my parents and she complains about me. It's not mature, but neither of us is at our best. I don't have the words to explain that I'm jealous of her. That I would die to be in her position: college degree, married, with a baby on the way. She and her husband are living with my parents so they can save for their house. They're building the life I always dreamed about. She feels like I'm sucking up all the air in the room—like I'm taking something away from her—and she's frustrated. But she has a real partner. A father for her baby. All I have is a boyfriend I have to text in secret and a mom who keeps looking over at me, sighing, and saying, "I can't believe you did this. I mean, really, Mayci? I taught you better than this." It feels like she keeps forgetting I'm pregnant. She's in shock that this is our new reality.

I HAVEN'T BEEN TO any prenatal appointments other than the one at the Pregnancy Resource Center in Provo. I want Arik to be with me for my first real ultrasound. I have my mom, which I'm grateful for, but I know that nobody will be as excited to see the baby's heartbeat as Arik. He's the person who should stand beside the bed with me. He's the person who should laugh when I have to rub the slimy gel off my stomach. But my parents are totally opposed to him coming. It's nonnegotiable.

The appointment is only supposed to be a couple minutes long, but I wait for over an hour to see the doctor. He looks like he's in his fifties, with a graying beard and obviously dyed hair. He's impatient—I feel like I'm wasting his time. He has a reputation for being good at C-sections. I don't want a C-section, but my mom had four, and my sister Lauren's pregnancy ended in one, so everyone assumes I'm going to have to get one too.

In the car on the drive home, I text Arik that I saw the heartbeat again. I send a Snapchat of the ultrasound. The baby has her arms crossed. I tell Arik the situation this baby is being born into is so messed up that she's probably praying in the womb.

THIRTY-ONE

I'M SITTING WITH MY DAD OUTSIDE OUR CHURCH. I'M SUPposed to go inside to meet the new bishop so I can begin repenting and earn my ecclesiastical endorsement back, but I'm nervous. I don't have a great history of meeting with bishops.

Beside me, my dad unbuckles his seat belt and says, "You ready?"

"Sure," I say.

In the bishop's office, I sit in one of the chairs that are pressed against the wall, expecting him to take a seat on the other side of the large desk.

Instead, he takes the chair next to me, so I have to turn to see his face. He's so close to me that I can practically smell his breath. The door is closed and we're alone. I tell him I have a lot to repent for—almost two years of sins. I know the conversation is going to be uncomfortable, but after my experience with the BYU faculty I expect the bishop to be understanding. He's not. When I begin to talk about Dick, he interrupts me and says I'm not taking responsibility for my actions.

"I'm trying to," I say.

I tell him I didn't consent to having sex for the first time. I explain that Dick and I were drinking together; that the last thing I remember about that night is lifting my cup to my lips. I'm still in denial about the way I had my virginity taken from me, so I don't use the word "rape." But I make it clear that I didn't consent to what happened.

The bishop makes me feel like a slut, like I'm the perpetrator. He says that since I kept sleeping with Dick after that night, I obviously consented. And then he says I should consider giving Arik's and my baby up for adoption. He has this whole story about someone in his family who was adopted.

I think adoption is great. Arik was adopted. But I don't know if I want to give my baby up. And I don't like the way the bishop is talking to me.

He starts naming my sins and counting them on his fingers: having sex, smoking weed, drinking coffee. He faces me again, holding up my sins on his fingers, and asks, in this super serious voice, "Have you had tea?"

"I guess so," I say. "I don't really drink tea. But maybe, like, one time?"

"You're not even sad about all this," he says, disappointed. "You don't feel sorry about anything you've done. You're not showing remorse."

I do feel remorse, so much that it's debilitating at times. But I've already told so many people about all of this—Lauren, my dad, my mom, BYU athletics. This guy is really far down the list. I don't have any tears left to cry. And even if I did, I really don't want to get emotional in front of this douchebag.

He goes on a rant about how his son didn't get into BYU. He says I'm taking worthy tithing-payers' scholarship money away because I'm not following the rules. He says, "I have no problem not giving you your endorsement to go back to BYU."

The conversation ends after an hour. He says I need to see him weekly.

I walk out and get in my dad's car. The second I shut the door, I start sobbing. I don't tell my dad that the bishop blamed me for getting assaulted. I don't want to unload that on my dad. But I tell him that talking to the bishop was one of the worst experiences of my entire life; that he told me everything that happened was my fault, that he said I wasn't showing remorse just because I wasn't crying.

My dad says, "If he tries to take your scholarship away, I'll be pissed and step in."

THIRTY-TWO

MY DAD TALKS TO ARIK'S PARENTS ON THE PHONE. THEY say that if I decide to give up the baby for adoption, they'd want to keep it. My dad says absolutely not.

I wish he'd be easier on them. They're still offering me and Arik their condo in Provo. Part of me wants to take them up on it. Arik and I could raise the baby together. Jeff and Liz could help. It would be so much nicer than being stuck in Coto, fighting with my parents.

But I know I can't actually do it. I'm a Jones. I belong here. I need to fix my mistakes.

Still, I feel trapped. I snap at my mom when she mentions again that she can't believe I got pregnant, I snip at McCall, and when my dad knocks on my bedroom door one evening after dinner, I look up at him and say, "What?" like a bratty teenager.

He's holding a black journal. Big, with a hard cover. He tells me I should write about this time in my life. "The good, the bad, the ugly." He looks around my room: the pile of clothes on the floor, the textbooks stacked on my desk, the half-empty suitcase. "Write everything down," he continues. "When you're mad at McCall, at Mom, at me. Detail your experience." He steps farther into my room. "Who knows? Maybe one day you'll write a book and it'll help someone else."

I've never thought of myself as a writer. And I don't want any more homework. I throw the journal in the corner of my room and try to forget about it.

But a couple days later, I open it and write, "It's been three weeks since I have been home and I still don't even have any words to say." I write about feeling trapped, about how I never have a moment alone anymore. "I try my best to stay positive, but sometimes I just want to crack." My parents are always watching me. I can't leave the house without three people asking where I'm going. It's claustrophobic.

It feels stupid to tell all of this to a journal. But I find I like writing. It feels good. Each time I sit down at my desk, I think about my future. One day, I tell myself, I'll have a good life and write about how everything that's happened was so shitty and how I turned my life around and proved everyone wrong. One day, I'll be with Arik and I'll turn this whole thing into a book. It becomes my first real dream since leaving BYU. The first glimmer of light.

In my journal, I chronicle my weekly meetings with the bishop, and how I don't know how to articulate how much I love Arik. When people ask me about him, I don't know where to start. With his personality? His eyes? The way he makes me feel free?

We're still FaceTiming and texting, but in secret, because my dad gets angrier with him by the day. He's started investigating him. He wants to prove to me that Arik's a bad guy. This is awful for me, because Arik and I are talking about getting married, maybe even in June. I'm like, *Why would I leave Arik without a reason? Who wants to be a single mom?* I love Arik. I know he's a little messy and chaotic, but so am I.

My dad and I fight about this. We both get loud. During one argument, my dad says, "I would bet my entire house that Arik cheated on you." He's sitting behind his desk in his office. I'm standing across from him, looking at the back of his desktop and the pictures he keeps of me, Alex, Lauren, and McCall.

He's got one of me hitting backhand as a four-year-old and another, with the same form, as a teenager. I feel so far away from those versions of myself.

I look away from them and say, "You're wrong."

But when I go upstairs and shut the door to my bedroom, I text Arik. I want to know if he's ever cheated on me. If there's anything I should know. He says no. Of course not. He gets defensive and texts me a paragraph about how I'm looking for the bad, then he mails red roses to the house, which I display downstairs, where everyone can see them.

MY DAD ENLISTS LAUREN to help him look into Arik. He wants to overturn every stone in Arik's life. Lauren agrees, and she asks the girls on the team to talk. At first, everyone protects me, but when she presses them, they start to open up.

My teammates talk about seeing Arik getting drunk at parties. Everything Lauren learns, she tells my dad: including the name of the other girl Arik got pregnant.

Lauren and my dad both call her. My dad calls her parents, too, then signs into my mom's Facebook and sends messages to all of Arik's ex-girlfriends.

I feel crazy and embarrassed. My parents want me to keep my pregnancy a secret, but they're calling half of Utah to ask about Arik.

And I'm starting to get more and more suspicious of him too.

ONE NIGHT, ARIK AND I have a three-way call with a girl my dad thinks Arik cheated on me with. It's my idea to all speak together. I've talked to the girl on my own, but the things she's saying aren't adding up. I want her and Arik to hash it out in front of me. I sit at my desk in my sweats, conference the two of them into a call, and say, "You guys talk," then stay on the line and listen. It's so awkward that I almost start laughing. The girl tears into Arik. They go back and forth. In the end, I believe Arik and not the girl, mainly because the girl says she doesn't know if she and Arik slept together when we were dating. She says she'd need to ask her roommate.

When I hang up, I feel exhausted. I wish Arik didn't have such a messy past. I wish my parents could chill out. I hate that this is how I'm spending my pregnancy. I should be shopping for strollers and picking out baby names, not DMing random girls to ask if they got drunk and slept with my boyfriend while we were dating.

    I go downstairs, where my dad is sitting in his study sticking printouts of text exchanges and photos of Arik's Instagram posts in a manila folder. I tell him that Arik might have some growing up to do, but that he's a good person. I show him the text Arik sent my doubles partner, Tara, where he wrote, "I will always be there for her and I will love her for all eternity." But my dad ignores this. He can't see the way Arik makes me laugh, or how free I feel when I'm with him. All he can see is that his youngest daughter is unmarried, pregnant, and dating a boy he doesn't approve of.

THIRTY-THREE

NEAR THE END OF MY FIRST TRIMESTER, MY MOM, MCCALL, and I drive to San Francisco to watch BYU play the University of San Francisco. The whole way, my mom and McCall tell me that Arik's bad news. That I shouldn't marry him. That we need to break up. I haven't made up my mind about anything yet, including adoption, but I'm leaning toward keeping the baby and staying with Arik. I really think I want to marry him, even though my dad's investigation is getting to me. I don't want to admit it to myself, but I'm starting to have real doubts.

When my mom and McCall aren't lecturing me about Arik, the three of us listen to the podcast *Serial*. To this day, hearing its theme song makes me sick. It reminds me of that drive—of my family harping on Arik and me worrying they might be right.

The matches that weekend take place at the Olympic Club. Players' parents have come to watch, and they elbow each other when I walk into the stands. We've kept my pregnancy secret from our ward in California, but almost everyone associated with BYU tennis knows. I try to ignore the stares, but it's hard. I've gone from being a star to an outcast.

That night, I lay awake in my hotel room and listen to a song for the music class I'm taking. It's the closing aria of the opera *Dido and Aeneas* called "When I'm Laid in the Earth." I've never heard it before, but listening to it, I get this eerie feeling. It reminds me of my grandma, an opera singer who went to Juilliard. But it's more than that. The song is about Aeneas falling in love with Dido but leaving her. She's so upset that she sets herself on fire so he can see that she's killed herself.

Listening to it, I remember leaving Arik in Utah, and the way he pulled me against him in the parking lot. I start crying. I have a feeling that something bad is going to happen.

BACK IN ORANGE COUNTY, my parents tell me they want me to see a Latter Day Saints therapist. They don't really believe in therapy, but they're worried about me. They don't think I have a handle on the situation. And they think the therapist can help me decide if I should keep the baby or give her up for adoption.

The four of us do a session together, and then I go alone two more times. I like therapy. I can finally say how I feel.

After each session, my mom asks, "What did you talk about?"

I say, "Well, it's private, so—"

"Come on, Mayci," she pushes me.

"I'm not sharing anything with you, Mom."

MY DAD ASKS ME to come to his office. He says he knows Arik cheated on me. As I stare at the Instagram post my dad printed out with a familiar girl's name in the comments, I know I need to look into it. But I also know it's not proof.

I say so to my dad, but he's insistent. For an hour we talk about whether Arik cheated on me. I say over and over again that I trust Arik, that I know he wouldn't hurt me, that he loves me, but when I go back upstairs, I climb into my bed and cry in big, heaving sobs, because I think my dad might be right.

Arik definitely lied to me. He was absolutely sus. I think about the night I was in Denver, when he was so vague and strangely loving over text. I think about the time he didn't call me back on Halloween, and the evening I cooked him dinner and he never showed up. None of these moments felt super meaningful before. But I look back at the messages I sent him that night I was in Denver—how I wrote, "I feel no love from you whatsoever," and, "I feel sketched out knowing your prob with hoes doing God knows what and that's why you take a millennium to respond"—and I wonder: why haven't I listened to my gut? Part of me believes it's because I didn't want to know. I felt so free in this relationship. I couldn't bear to second-guess it. Another part of me knows that what I love about Arik is his spontaneity: the way we can wrestle or play hide-and-seek like little kids. But what if his chaotic energy wasn't made to be contained by a relationship?

I've never felt so depressed. I pull the covers over my head, my eyes streaming. I want someone to medicate me so I feel less alone, but I don't think I can take antidepressants while pregnant. I press a hand to my stomach, hoping that feeling the baby will make me feel less alone. But there's nothing, just a hard lump.

THIRTY-FOUR

IN THE MORNING, MY DAD LEAVES FOR A BUSINESS TRIP. I get up, my head pounding, and move to my desk. Tucking my feet under me, I push aside my textbooks, open my laptop, and look through Arik's old photos on Instagram.

So many girls have commented on his posts. One asked him to hang out the night I was in Denver. I reach out to Arik's cousin Brian to ask about her. Brian doesn't drink, so he'll remember if Arik cheated on me with the girl in question. And he likes me. I know that if I tell him what's going on, he'll give me the truth.

Brian confirms that Arik cheated on me when I was in Denver—not with the girl in the comments but with her friend—meaning the day before I found out I was pregnant, the day he texted me, "Love you so much I promise," he was having a drunken one-night stand with someone else.

"I'm sorry, Mayc," Brian says on the phone. He sounds gutted. I don't feel that bad for him. If my cousin was blackout drunk and I knew he had a girlfriend, I might've tried to stop him from sleeping with someone else. I might've intervened.

I hang up and call the girl. I tell her who I am, that I'm pregnant, that I need to know if Arik cheated. She admits that she slept with Arik that night. She says they were drunk and that she didn't know he had a girlfriend, but when I look at her page, I see we have mutual friends. I'm still not mad at her. I'm mad at Arik.

I feel like I'm going to throw up. I can't believe Arik did this. And I hate that my dad was right.

I don't tell him what's going on. Instead, I text Arik and tell him I want to FaceTime. I do my hair and makeup so he can see what he's losing.

When he answers, he tells me he's alone. His parents are in Wasatch at his brother's baseball game. He knows my dad has been researching him, so he's already on edge. I ask him if he cheated on me. He says no. I ask again. He says no again. He says I should talk to Brian. I tell him I already did and that Brian told me the truth.

Arik breaks down. He says, "Mayci, I fucked up. I'm so sorry."

I tell him he'll never do better than me. Our baby will never call him Daddy because he or she will have a new dad. I end the conversation by saying, "You're going to be paying me child support every month, so have a good fucking life." I don't say it to be cruel. I just want him to feel like he's losing me. I want him to feel the sting of betrayal the way I do.

When I hang up, I pick up a picture frame that's been on my desk and throw it at the window, damaging the shutters, then leave the glass on the floor and call Arik's dad. Jeff's been so supportive. I want him to hear what happened from me. I don't want Arik to be able to tell his parents that I broke up with him for no reason. I want the Macks to know that Arik cheated on me.

Jeff and I talk for over an hour. I'm crying so hard I can barely catch my breath. Jeff tells me I'm the first girl he's seen Arik really love. That it's real. He encourages me to keep an open mind. He says Arik and I love each other. We can work it out. He's not trying to convince me to get back together with Arik, but he doesn't think I would've called him if I didn't love Arik. He thinks I should consider giving Arik a second chance.

While we're on the phone, Arik sends me a photo. It's a mirror selfie of us. I'm wearing black leggings and a black top. Arik's hugging me in a striped gray tank. The bathroom sink is cluttered. It's a moment from a busy and different life.

TOLD YOU SO

I write back, "I'm confused as to why you would send this to me. What is the purpose honestly I'm just confused."

Arik responds saying that he loves me. I deserve better. He'll never forgive himself. He's sorry he put me through this. The text ends on the letter *J*. It's unfinished.

THIRTY-FIVE

MY MOM IS STANDING IN MY DOORWAY. SHE'S WEARING her typical weekday outfit: jeans and a white scoop-neck. Makeup on, hair blown out and straight.

I tell her that Dad was right. Arik cheated on me.

"I hate him," I tell her, ripping off the diamond necklace he gave me for my birthday. The chain snaps in half and the charm flies off. I sink onto the bed, where my mom gives me a hug.

"We have to get you out of the house," she says.

I don't want to go anywhere, but I follow her down the stairs and out to the car. We don't talk on the drive to get Mexican food. To calm my rage and anxious thoughts, I scroll Instagram. I feel so far away from BYU. So far away from tennis. So far away from myself. And there's this strange feeling in my stomach. Almost a fluttering.

It takes ten minutes to get to the taco place. The whole drive, I feel like I'm in shock. I can't believe that Arik cheated on me. I can't believe that if I don't give this baby up for adoption, I'm going to be a single mom.

My ego is crushed. I'm like, *Me? Mayci Jones? Cheated on? How is this real life?*

Inside the restaurant, I pull myself together enough to order, then I sit at a table and look at my phone again. I know I'm not going to find what I'm looking for on the internet, but it's a good distraction to scroll past other people's pictures of nights out and curated lifestyles. I can't believe I used to have anything to post about. I can't believe I ever trusted Arik.

I'm thinking about him when I see a picture of him and a cousin. The caption reads, "RIP Arik Mack." I think it's a sick joke. Something to get my attention. I scroll past it and see another photo: one of a mutilated truck in Spanish Fork Canyon. There's a caption: "One person died after a semi truck carrying coal rolled on US-6 Tuesday afternoon, officials said." The picture is horrible. Glass and twisted metal strewn across the road.

I feel frantic. Sick. I look up at my mom, unable to speak. My phone rings. It's one of Arik's friends, calling to ask if Arik is actually dead. Sobbing, I try to call Arik. Maybe it's a dream. Maybe it's all a joke. I pray that I'll hear his voice, that he'll answer, that he'll explain everything. The phone rings and rings, but he doesn't pick up. Nobody does. I call him again and again.

I stand and run out of the restaurant. I feel so dizzy I might pass out. I grab hold of a trash can, my whole body shaking, and wait for my mom to help me into the car.

That's when I call Arik's dad. I'm sobbing before he answers. He sounds calm, measured. He tells me Arik passed away in a car crash. He doesn't want me to worry because he doesn't want anything to hurt the baby. I tell him I'm sorry—over and over again—while my mom cries in the driver's seat beside me.

I blame myself for Arik's death. He was texting me. I made him upset. I feel responsible. I can't stop playing the what-if game. If I had texted him back, what would've happened? If I had forgiven him, would he have gone for that drive? If I hadn't been so cruel on the phone, would anything have been different?

I feel a pain I didn't know was possible. I don't know how to go on.

I call Lauren. I tell her Arik is dead.

"What?" she says.

I tell her again, screaming the words. She's confused—we were on the phone an hour and a half earlier when I was crying that Arik had cheated on me. This is too much for either of us to process.

Back home, my mom parks in our driveway, and I follow her into the house. It feels impossible that it's still standing—the same chandelier hanging in the entryway, same curving staircase, same medallion in the middle of the travertine floor.

I go to the couch, where McCall sits with me and cries. I assume she feels bad for being so mean to me. I look up articles about the crash. Arik was thrown from his car and went through the windshield. He died immediately.

My brother gets home from work and brings tart frozen yogurt with strawberries, which is the only food I can stomach.

Nobody will let me go up to my room. They all want to watch me. I sit between them on the couch, hunched over my phone. Everyone is posting about Arik. And everyone wants to follow me. Arik and I were never Instagram official, but we've posted Snapchats together, and he did an Instagram post for my birthday in February, so people have put it together. They want the drama—they already know I left BYU, just not exactly why. I don't want to give them anything. I make my Instagram private.

My brother sees me sobbing and offers to give me a priesthood blessing—a prayer for people in distress. I sit in a chair while he lays his hands over my head. It's comforting. He cries afterward, which surprises me. I don't think I've ever seen Alex cry.

Afterward, we watch *Beverly Hills Ninja* because my siblings think it will keep me from crying and looking up news articles about Arik. I can't focus. I feel pressured to say something on Instagram. People who don't even know Arik are posting about him. So are the girls I've talked to as part of my dad's investigation. It's like everyone has assigned themselves a eulogy at his funeral. I look at my feed, feeling guilty for refusing to ever let Arik write a caption about me. Then I post, "Out of all the pictures we have together, this is one of my favorites. Not the most attractive one, but it shows how we were: Happy. You kept on asking me when I was going to post a picture with you and I am sorry I didn't post sooner. My heart is completely broken right now, I cannot even begin to say how sad I am right now and I can't even imagine life without you."

I write about how I'm going to miss waking up to his good-morning texts, and talking to him, and movie nights with the worst picks, and late-night Frosty runs, and his ridiculous Albert Einstein hair.

The second I post, people start texting, commenting, and calling. I look between my phone and the TV. There are rumors going around that there was a second person in the car. And one station is showing an aerial view of the accident: a semicircle of police cruisers around Arik's body, which is covered in a blue plastic drape. Seeing this, and images of the car we'd had so many memories in completely destroyed, shatters me. I feel sick that he died alone, with no one there to hold him or allow him to say goodbye.

My mom and Alex tell me to turn off the TV, but I can't. Each time a newscaster talks about the traffic from the accident, I want to scream, *Do you know* why *there's traffic? Arik wasn't nobody. He's the father of my baby. This isn't some random person—this is someone I love!*

My mom touches my arm and says she wants me to sleep in her room tonight. She wants to keep an eye on me.

"Fine," I say.

I don't care. I lie on a twin mattress on the floor beside her bed and alternate staring at my phone and ceiling all night. Suddenly I'm sure I'm going to have a boy. I don't know why. I just feel it.

THIRTY-SIX

I GO BACK TO THE OB-GYN. I NEED TO KNOW IF I'M HAVING a boy or a girl. I need to be able to tell Arik's parents at the funeral.

My mom, McCall, and my sister-in-law Katelyn come with me. When I check in, a nurse takes me to a room, where she weighs me. I've lost five pounds from the stress, which is bad news. I sit on the paper sheet and wait for the doctor. He knocks on the door, his white coat on, then walks in and asks what happened.

I tell him that Arik died.

He has me lie back and puts a warm gel on my stomach. I'm only thirteen and a half weeks along, so it's hard to find the baby's sex. He tries for a couple minutes, then brings in a woman who takes a turn with the ultrasound machine.

She tells me, almost instantly, that I'm having a boy. Arik and I were sure we were having a girl. But once he died, I knew in my soul it was a boy. I take a breath, then sob.

As I'm sitting up and wiping my cheeks my mom tells the doctor, "Mayci's son's father had a lot of partners, if you know what I mean." She makes a face. It's so awkward in the room. I want to die. She could've just told the doctor that I need a simple STD test. Instead, she's made it so weird.

Nobody says anything for a moment, and the doctor tells me they can do a blood draw to check.

Afterward, as we're leaving the office, I feel dizzy. I keep visualizing Arik's car on the road. The hallway goes black. I reach for the nearest wall, unsteady. When I open my eyes, I'm on the ground, surrounded by nurses and doctors. I let them help me onto a bed, then lie there and think about Arik: How I yelled at him an hour before he veered into that semi-truck. How the instant I heard about the crash, none of the cheating or lying mattered. How I wish I'd never said any of it. How I wish I could go back in time.

LATER THAT DAY, MY dad gets back from his business trip. My mom, McCall, and I pick him up at the airport. While we idle outside the terminal, he tells me to get out of the car. I climb out, he hugs me, and he says he's sorry. We all cry.

My dad had been so hard on Arik. But he knew I loved him. He knew I wanted to marry him and raise a child with him. He never says "I told you so," never brings up the conversation where he said he'd bet his house that Arik had cheated on me.

He just pulls me against him, like I'm a kid again.

When we get back to the house, he helps me study for the finance test I have to take the next day.

We sit at the kitchen table. Someone's left the buffalo sauce out. I start bawling when I see it. Arik knew I loved buffalo sauce and had bought a bottle to keep at his apartment. Everything I see reminds me of him. I can't keep it together.

THE NEXT DAY, I take my finance test at a college in the area. I have to pass the exam to stay NCAA eligible, but I can't stop picturing Arik's hands on the steering wheel. I wonder if he was thinking about our fight or listening to one of our songs. The idea of him playing the song he texted me when I tried to break up with him for Liam makes me want to scream. I squeeze my eyes shut, then open them and stare at the papers in front of me.

Later, when I'm home, I see an Instagram post about how you'll know you were meant to be a mom when you lock eyes with your baby and see their precious soul. Reading the caption, I know without a doubt I'm keeping this baby. Some people's challenge is needing to do IVF and not being able to get pregnant. Mine is getting pregnant by accident and losing my baby's father. *At least I won't ever have to do IVF*, I think to myself.

I walk into my parents' room and sit in the armchair next to their fireplace. "I'm keeping the baby," I tell my mom. "We're made for each other. I feel it."

THIRTY-SEVEN

I FLY TO UTAH FOR ARIK'S FUNERAL. EVERYTHING REMINDS me of him: the mountains, the freeway exit I'd take to get to his apartment, the place where we'd get breakfast burritos at three a.m. I can't imagine loving anyone else as much as I loved him. And I can't imagine anyone wanting me ever again. I feel heartbroken—like I'll never be OK again.

My parents take me straight to Liz and Jeff's house for an open-casket viewing. I'm so anxious. I don't want to see Arik's body. I don't think I'll be able to handle it. There are grown men sobbing on the steps outside the house.

Arik's dad lets me in through a side door so I don't have to see the casket. He hugs me for a long time and I sob. My dad cries too. I can only remember him crying twice before all of this. He's always been more logical than emotional. My pregnancy and Arik's death have softened him. It's softened all of us.

Lauren and my parents don't stay for the viewing. I think they want to let me have time with Arik's family. It's hard to imagine that just a month ago Lauren and my dad wouldn't even let me see Arik. That he and I had to say our goodbye in a parking lot. It's hard to believe that was the last time we were together.

Inside, it feels almost like a celebration: everyone's laughing and telling funny stories. Arik's brother gives me Arik's dog tag, which is scratched from the crash. I run my fingers along the roman numerals I had engraved on the back, then place it in the pocket of my jeans and know I'll take it to the hospital with me when I give birth.

Talking and reminiscing with Arik's friends and relatives is almost fun. I feel like Arik is with me; like he's with all of us. I meet Arik's aunts and uncles, who tell me how happy they are that I'm carrying his baby. It's odd to me that only now, when Arik's dead, can people feel happy that I'm pregnant. But I'm so relieved to be around this energy. I didn't think anyone would celebrate an "unwanted pregnancy."

After an hour, Arik's parents take me to their back office to talk. I've never been there before. We sit across from each other. I've been waiting to tell them I'm having a boy. I brought the ultrasound photo to Utah and everything.

I ask them if they think the baby is a boy or a girl.

"A boy," Liz says immediately.

We look at the ultrasound together. It feels like an alternate reality—I keep thinking about what this would've been like if Arik were alive.

After a half hour, we go back out. The viewing is ending. People are hugging one another as they go out to their cars. It's strange to see grown men sobbing with their heads between their legs.

ARIK'S CASKET IS DARK brown. His parents have placed his high school baseball jersey across the top. I walk toward it, Jeff and Liz practically holding me up as I hyperventilate.

"Are you ready?" Liz asks.

I nod, my breath coming in sobs, and she and Jeff leave the room. I want to crawl inside the casket and lie next to Arik. Instead, when the door shuts, I fall onto the casket, bawling. I tell Arik that I love him, that I'm sorry, that I forgive him, that I'm having a boy. "I assume you know that," I say. And then, "I love you. Watch over us."

THIRTY-EIGHT

THE FUNERAL IS ON A SATURDAY. I WEAR A NEW BLACK dress my mom bought me. It's the first time I really notice my bump. I'm self-conscious of it. It's one thing for Arik's family to know that I'm having his baby, but my parents have asked me to keep my pregnancy quiet. That's fine with me—I don't want more rumors circulating after his funeral. I plan to spend the entire day sucking my stomach in.

The church is full. We're early, but almost all the seats are taken, and we find a few together in the back. There are big photographs of Arik on the walls. I look at them and start sobbing right away. My mom tries to calm me down because she's worried about the baby. I'm almost hyperventilating again. I can't seem to catch my breath.

During Arik's dad's speech, he names all the people who were instrumental in Arik's life. He hesitates before saying my name. "You were his soulmate," he chokes. "His soulmate." Beside me, my dad stiffens, upset. I feel like I might split in half.

After the speeches, we watch a hearse take Arik's body away. I can't hold back my tears. I know it's the last time I'll see him. It's gutting.

LATER, THERE'S LUNCH IN another church building. I sob on and off, too exhausted and sad to feel embarrassed. My fake eyelashes have peeled off. My back hurts from sucking in my bump. Everything about this day has been a nightmare. My son won't have a dad in his life. Arik is gone. I'm alone.

I TAKE A BREAK from journaling. I have nothing to say. Every day feels like a chore. I think about dying, then feel guilty—like I'm failing myself and failing Arik.

I don't go back to the LDS therapist. I don't know if she can help me. Instead, I look at pictures of myself as a little kid. In one, I'm wearing a white dress with silver stars and holding a rose. I barely recognize that little girl. I can't imagine being that happy or innocent ever again. I know I'm depressed. But I've always thought of depression as a choice. How I feel now is not a choice. I'm afraid I'm going to hurt myself or my baby. Each time my family says something negative about Arik, I fume inside. Every night, I fall asleep sobbing over pictures and videos of the two of us together. It's like an addiction. All I want to do is remember him, read our texts, and dream about him.

When my mom and I watch *Interstellar*, I break down. Arik loved space. *Interstellar* was one of his favorite movies. All I can think about, watching Matthew McConaughey leave an inhospitable Earth, is going to the Clark Planetarium with Arik. How we'd played hide-and-seek and acted like little kids. I wonder when everything won't remind me of him. I think about him every second of every day, which is torture, but at the same time, it's all I want to do.

I HAVE TO SEE the bishop. I don't want to go. He's the last person on Earth I want to talk to about Arik. But I need to show up and play the part to get my endorsement back.

When I get to the church, he asks me to tell him what happened to Arik. I know he wants the gossip. He's leaning forward in his chair.

I cry, because it's all I've been doing lately.

He smiles and says, "It's nice to see you showing some emotion."

TOLD YOU SO

ARIK'S BIRTHDAY IS APRIL 8. Two weeks after the crash. Instagram is flooded with girls talking about how sad they are that he's dead. The girl I had been on a three-way call with posts a picture of herself wearing a hat with Arik's last name on it. It's interesting to me that she's proudly shouting about him for her Instagram followers to see when she had been so quick to make him look bad just a couple weeks ago.

She wasn't the one he cheated on me with, but I stare at her pictures anyway and wonder why he cheated. Was I not pretty enough? Not skinny enough? Did he ever really love me? I feel like the ugly, massive outcast—afraid of running into people and tired of hiding my pregnancy, even though I'm not even halfway through. I think about how my sisters are both perfect and I'm the fuckup. The daughter who hears "I told you so" again and again because she has to learn everything the hard way. I'm getting chubby. My skin is bad. I worry I'll be alone for the rest of my life.

Living feels impossible. It takes so much effort for me to brush my teeth, to shower, to eat. Anytime I laugh, I start sobbing. My emotions are all over the place. I don't know how to hide them anymore.

ONE NIGHT, I DREAM that Arik is visiting me from heaven. We only have a little bit of time. We catch up, and then he leaves through a vibrant line of yellow trees—the same ones I have a photo of him walking through. When I look back at the picture, I realize he's in a cemetery. How did I never notice that before?

The next morning, I write in my journal, "It hurts. More than anything I have ever experienced. I wish I could go back in time and save him, tell him not to drive up the canyon, tell him I love him one last time. I miss him so much that sometimes it is unbearable. He was my best friend, he was my everything. To lose that is just unfathomable." Then I close my journal and look at happy couples on Instagram. The more time I spend online, the unhappier I get. But I can't stop.

MAYCI NEELEY

MY MOM TELLS ME she's sorry she called me a slut. We're in the car.

"It's OK," I say, after a moment.

I can't remember any time she's apologized before. I have never been great at apologizing either. It seems to be a trait we all have in the Jones family.

"I was angry," she says.

"I know," I tell her. "I get it. I'm angry too."

That night, I lie awake and look at my old messages with Arik again: the ones where he told me, "I see greatness in you, I see a person with potential to be a loving mother, a wise and spiritual leader for those in need of guidance. I want to marry you because our relationship was built upon friendship, love and compassion rather than the physical side of things—because you are my best friend and my motivation to do what's right."

I don't know how to think about this. I hate him for cheating on me and I hate him for lying about it, but I miss him so much. And I made mistakes too. Crying in bed, my arms wrapped around my stomach, I wish I could drink. One sip. It would make me feel so much better. It's the only thing that's helped numb the pain before.

THIRTY-NINE

MCCALL APPLIES TO THE ELLEN DEGENERES MOTHER'S Day Giveaway and is accepted. When she tells me at my parents' kitchen table, I want to apply, too, but it's past the deadline.

I fill out an online form with my story anyway: how Arik died when I was thirteen weeks pregnant; how I'm raising my baby as a single mom; how I want to go back to school and D1 tennis once he's born. It's the first pitch I write for myself.

I get a response later that day. An audience coordinator asks me how far along I am. When am I due? Am I having a boy or girl? Do I have a name yet? What do I do for a living? Am I married or single? What does my spouse do for a living?

I write back and say I'm fifteen weeks along. "I'm having a boy and I have not picked a name yet. I'm a student so I don't have a chosen career yet, so I have no income. I had a boyfriend but he passed away so I am single now."

The coordinator responds thanking me for my responses and says she's sorry for my loss. I should show up at the studio on Thursday at two, and I should bring my most recent sonogram. I'm going to be in the audience for the show.

WHEN I TELL MCCALL I'm going to the giveaway with her, I assume she'll be annoyed. I'm stealing her thunder again. But she's nice about it. We both know I need stuff for the baby, and I don't have any other way of getting it. My parents have money, but even though they're supporting me through my pregnancy, they've made it clear they're not just going to buy me everything for this baby.

The day of the show, McCall drives us to L.A., where we sit in the parking garage for over an hour, then walk across the street and into the studio, where we have to wait again. They assign us seats in different parts of the studio. I'm placed in the top-right corner, which I think is perfect, because it means nobody I know will recognize me on TV and find out that I'm pregnant. During the breaks, McCall and I hang out by the snack table. There's every different type of pregnancy craving laid out: pickles, cupcakes, little squares of cheddar cheese.

The giveaway is a turning point for me. I go in with nothing and leave with a crib, a year's supply of diapers, gift cards, a stroller, and a baby swing—all the baby gear I didn't know I needed, plus all of the things I imagined I'd need but didn't know how I'd afford. I also leave feeling like I can do this. I can have this baby alone.

The feeling doesn't last long. My depression is constant. When my dad has a business trip to Hawaii, my mom wants to go with him, but she's afraid I'll kill myself if she leaves me at home, so we all go and stay in one room.

I've been having awful dreams about Dick my whole pregnancy. In one, he finds out I'm pregnant with another man's baby, freaks out, and tries to kill me. In another, I've already had my baby, we're back together, and I'm trapped and terrified. When my parents mention Dick, I freak out and tell them not to say his name. It makes the dreams worse. It dawns on me that my grief for Arik is entangled with the unhealed trauma from my relationship with Dick.

Hawaii, one of the most beautiful places in the entire world, is no match for any of this. I feel achingly alone while I'm there. Everything is meant for couples. And everything I see, particularly the beautiful sunsets, reminds me of Arik. I wonder how it's possible to feel so sad. My parents know I'm drowning in my depression, that I feel like I could break. But we don't actually talk about it.

In my journal, I write, "I just feel like I want to fall asleep and wake up next year or five years from now." Lying in bed later, listening to my parents laughing on the balcony, I tell myself I'll never go back to Hawaii. I hate it there.

THINGS AREN'T ANY BETTER at home. It's summer and hot in Orange County. My dad is too frugal to run the air-conditioning. It's not like he saves money in other arenas: he and my mom love going out to eat, and our family belongs to one of the country clubs in Coto de Caza. But he acts like turning the AC below eighty degrees is going to set his retirement back five years.

When I sit in my bedroom studying, sweat runs down my chest. It's literally a stream from my boobs to my thighs. I'm huge now. I'm sticky all over. And I can feel the skin on my thighs ripping and itching with stretch marks.

I start going to the library more, mostly because it's cold there. But it's also the only place my mom lets me go alone. I think she assumes I can't kill myself on the ten-minute drive between our house and the Mission Viejo Public Library. Joke's on her—I definitely could. But I don't. I'm taking three more classes: Child Development, LDS Temples, and Mission Prep. When I bend over my laptop to study, my belly resting on my legs, I wonder whose life I'm living. I don't feel anything like the girl who won national tennis tournaments, or went out dancing with her friends and boyfriend, or whose poster was all over campus at BYU.

FORTY

I'M STANDING ON THE EDGE OF A BOAT, LOOKING OUT AT the water. It's dark blue and rippling. Behind me, vacationers are having fun: drinking, laughing, and dancing as our cruise ship sails from Florida to the Dominican Republic. I want to be happy so badly, but I'm miserable. I step closer to the railing and imagine jumping off. Then my baby kicks, and I know I need to be strong for him. I know I can't kill myself. Not now, at least.

My mom knows there's something wrong with me. She's everywhere. She makes me sleep in the room with her and my dad and follows me all over the ship.

We don't talk about the fact that my mom thinks I'm going to hurt myself. But it's right there, under the surface. When she accompanies me into the bathroom, both of us wearing dresses for dinner, we take a mirror selfie. I'm holding the phone in my right hand, my left arm dangling limply beside my hip. She has one hand on my shoulder, the other clasping my bump, like she's doing her best to keep me here. We both are.

One afternoon, we take a speedboat to a nearby island. There's a snack table laid out with pineapple and chips. I eye the makeshift bar. The alcohol is free, which means by not drinking, my family is leaving money on the table. I imagine sneaking a series of shots so I don't have to be in my head anymore. My mom sees me standing beside the alcohol and waves me over.

I don't want to sit with her. I couldn't care less if I live or die. I feel terrible for thinking this, because I know plenty of people have it worse than me. I have my mom, who has come to every doctor's appointment with me, and my dad, who's there for me each time I study for a finance exam. I have my room in my parents' house, where I feel safe (and a little sweaty). And I have Lauren, who tells me I can come back to tennis, that having a baby doesn't mean my life is over. But some days it doesn't feel like enough. Some days I want to take a shot of rum to numb my pain, and then I want to die.

I know that's selfish. But I can't help it.

MY MOM AND I fly to Utah. I need to fill out paperwork to prepare for my return to BYU. It feels insane to think about playing tennis again when my stomach is the size of a bowling ball, but I follow my mom around campus, ducking my head when I see anyone who might recognize me. The thought of running into someone is horrific—but there's a part of me that's happy to be back in Utah. I feel at home here. I like seeing the mountains, driving to Swig, and visiting the places I was happy with Arik. I feel him with me when I'm in Utah. And I start to look for God more. I'm becoming more spiritual. I need religion to help make everything make sense.

One afternoon, my mom and I get lunch with Arik's family. His dad is too thin. It seems to me that he's really struggling. When we sit down to eat at Malawi's Pizza, he can barely speak. It's like his spirit isn't in his body.

Liz carries the conversation. She asks me how I'm doing; how the baby is. Every once in a while, Jeff smiles, but he doesn't say anything.

I feel terrible for him and less sorry for myself. I can't imagine what it's like to lose a child. I'm devastated by Arik's death, and I knew him less than a year. For Liz and Jeff, this must be unbearable. I have no idea how they're keeping it together.

When I get in the car with my mom after lunch, I tell myself I'm going to be stronger. That, for Arik and my baby, I'm not going to let loss define me. My life isn't over, I can still become who I was meant to be and more.

TOLD YOU SO

A FEW DAYS LATER, my mom and I are driving the ten hours from Utah to California when her phone buzzes. My dad has texted.

"What is it?" I ask. She's clearly angry. "What?" I say again.

The bishop has told everyone in our ward that I'm pregnant. He assumes I'm going to be showing more soon, so it's better for everyone to know about the baby.

Anger washes over me. My mom's upset too. She's been creative with my outfits for months. It feels wrong that the bishop told everyone my secret after we've worked so hard to keep my pregnancy quiet. And we're both upset that my dad gave him permission to do it. I'm like, *You guys made me hide my pregnancy for six months, and then you let this guy I literally hate tell everyone about it?*

My mom's phone buzzes again. The women in our ward have started texting her. She's overwhelmed with messages. None of them are mean. They're all asking if we need support. But still—it's a lot.

I ask my mom if I can post my bump on Instagram now. "Everyone knows that I'm pregnant anyway. It'll be better if it's just out there."

"No," she says. She and my dad are worried it'll seem like bragging.

"It's not bragging," I say, looking at her in the driver's seat. "It's being honest and I'm tired of hiding it."

"It's not a good time," my mom says.

"Why?"

She tells me she's still worried going public will mess up my return to BYU.

FORTY-ONE

I STOP PLAYING TENNIS. MY PARENTS WANT ME TO WORK out and eat well, but it's hard.

All I want to do is eat bread and get Polar Pops with my dad. Only some gas stations have them, and there's no Swig in California. We go on little father-daughter outings to grab them, filling our Styrofoam cups with crushed ice and 44 ounces of Dr Pepper.

When I'm not taking my online classes or driving to get Polar Pops, my mom takes me to the movies. She's a busybody. She can't just sit in the house. She and I see basically every movie that comes out in 2015, just for something to do.

Sometimes, we stop at BuyBuy Baby on the way home. It's huge: there are dozens of aisles, towers of pacifiers, stacks of onesies, a million different bottles, and buzzing fluorescent lights overhead. I walk the aisles and look at the tiny clothes, the stuffed animals, the strollers and plastic baby baths and blankets.

It lets me imagine a future. It becomes my happy place.

TALKING TO MY FRIENDS makes me feel better too. I learn about their lives from my bed: Nicole's boyfriend, Tara's tennis success, Amy's relationship. We're in opposite stages of life. I'm grieving and pregnant while they're moving forward, but it works.

NEAR THE END OF my pregnancy, my doctor tells me I have too much amniotic fluid. It could be dangerous for the baby.

"What does that mean?" my mom asks. The doctor is on his way out of the exam room. He never spends more than a couple minutes with us.

"He might need a minor surgery after he's born."

"Surgery?" my mom repeats.

"You can google it," the doctor says, and leaves.

I look at my mom, my heart racing.

MY MOM HAD FOUR C-sections. Lauren had a C-section too. I don't want one. I can't even give blood without fainting. The idea of being cut open on an operating table is a nightmare. But my baby is big. At each appointment, my doctor tells me he's measuring one, two, three weeks ahead. My blood pressure is high too. I know this isn't good. I can feel it. My hands and feet look like they've been injected with helium. It's probably from all the buttery popcorn I've been eating at the movies with my mom.

I buy a blood-pressure cuff so I can take mine at home and pray I can give birth naturally. It feels like an insane wish. What I really want is to give birth with a partner, to have Arik in the room with me holding my hand. Since I can't have that, it seems like having the baby the way I want should be a given.

At every appointment—I have one every week now—I pray my baby won't have a stomach obstruction and that I won't be sliced open.

At thirty-six weeks, my baby is measuring thirty-nine weeks, with his belly in the 97th percentile and his head in the 98th. My doctor tells me he'll let me be induced a week early. But when I go in for my last ultrasound, the tech tells me the baby is too big for an induction. I need to schedule a C-section. I panic. I hope the baby will be OK, and that I'll feel Arik's presence when I'm in the operating room. He told me he would be there for me no matter what.

TOLD YOU SO

WHEN I WAKE UP on September 2 and realize it's the anniversary of the day Arik told me he loved me, I try to picture it. I lie in bed, staring at the ceiling, and replay the memory: the two of us cuddling, him saying, "Guess what?" his blue eyes piercing.

MY WATER BREAKS AT the hospital. I don't get a chance to ask anyone if I can try to birth naturally. I'm just told to walk down the hall for my C-section. In the operating room, I listen to one of my and Arik's songs while I get the spinal.

The needle feels like a bee sting, followed by pressure. I can't breathe. "Oxygen!" someone yells. Then they lay me down on the operating table. A monitor beeps, then another one. "Your oxygen level is one hundred percent," the anesthesiologist says, but I don't believe her. I panic. My blood pressure is dropping. I'm sure I'm going to die.

The surgery is easier, mainly because the nurse puts something to calm me down in my IV. I'm definitely not mad about it. My mom sits beside my head. I don't like the tugging, or the sounds of the operation. When the baby is out, I don't hear a cry. I can feel my heart racing. What if there's something wrong with him? But then there's a raspy cough. Then another. The doctor gently grasps my son's hand and uses it to wave *Hello, Mama*. Someone says the baby is perfect. He doesn't have a stomach obstruction. He won't need any surgery.

My mom cuts his cord, and then I'm holding him. My baby. He's wearing a beanie, white with pink and blue stripes. He's the most beautiful thing I've ever seen: warm and soft, with little rolls on his arms. I feel, lying on the operating table, like I could hold him forever. And then someone takes the baby to the recovery room, and I'm being sewn up. All seven layers are being put back together.

FORTY-TWO

SOMEONE FROM CHILD PROTECTIVE SERVICES COMES TO my hospital room. She asks my mom to leave. She wants to talk to me alone.

I sit in my hospital bed, the glue-lined incision along my lower stomach aching, as the woman asks me if I'm well enough to take the baby home. She knows about the situation with Arik. She says we don't know how giving birth is going to affect me. Will I be even more depressed? Will I be OK to be my baby's mom?

I look over at my son, asleep in his hospital bassinet. I want him more than I've ever wanted anything in my life. It's a relief to feel that way. To have a purpose.

I tell the CPS worker, "I'm happier than ever." And it's true.

When she leaves, I roll to my side and gingerly pick up my baby. As I bring him to my chest, I whisper his name: "Hudson Doutre Jones." My little savior.

ARIK'S FAMILY WANTS TO meet Hudson at the hospital. They're prepared with baby photos of Arik on their phones. We look at the pictures, and then at Hudson in his acrylic bassinet, trying to decide if Hudson looks like Arik. I can't tell what he looks like. Maybe a mix between us? He doesn't have Arik's name, because it would've upset my dad too much. I hope Jeff, Liz, and Jeff Jr. can see Arik in Hudson. I want them to have that.

We visit for a while, and then Liz stands to leave. Jeff and Jeff Jr. follow her lead.

"Thank you," Liz says, when she reaches the door. She tells me how much it meant to their family to meet Hudson.

I tell them how grateful I was for their support during my pregnancy. From the beginning, they welcomed me with open arms.

"I'll see you soon," I say, and then they're gone.

Once I'm alone, I reach into my diaper bag to hold the dog tag I had engraved for Arik; the one Jeff Jr. gave to me when I came to Utah for Arik's funeral.

It's not there. I throw everything out of the bag, scraping the bottom with my nails, but it's gone. Lost for good. I'm absolutely devastated. It was the one thing of his I had that was sentimental. I'd been planning to give it to Hudson.

I GO HOME AFTER four days in the hospital. Hudson is a perfect, easy baby. But there's something wrong with my incision. Each time I stand, it feels like it's going to tear open. I wonder if it's supposed to hurt this much. I go into the downstairs bathroom to investigate. The glue has ripped open. I can see a hole an inch wide and an inch deep in my abdomen. It's oozing blood and something slimy and yellow.

I feel like I'm going to throw up. I'm already on antibiotics for an infection I got from my pedicure. I wonder if I have a second one.

My mom calls the hospital. They refer me back to my OB, who can't see me until Monday.

I decide to stop taking my pain meds over the weekend. I want to know how much I'm pushing my body. Ever since Dick, I've been cautious around pills, and I've grown up knowing that my grandfather became addicted to the pain medication he was prescribed for his bad knees. I don't want to rely on any medication.

Instead, I fan my incision repeatedly. I wish I had one of those portable fans people use at Disneyland. Instead, I use my hand. Air is the only thing that stops the itching and burning. It's truly disgusting.

TOLD YOU SO

ON MONDAY, THE OB-GYN tells me to stick a Q-Tip covered in hydrogen peroxide into my incision and move it around. I hate everything about this, especially the fact that it doesn't work. After a week, my incision is just as infected as it was before. I need it to heal on schedule. It's almost October, and I'm supposed to be playing Division 1 tennis by January.

My mom finds a plastic surgeon who specializes in wound care. He packs my incision with gauze that I have to remove bit by bit. I do, and gradually I start to heal.

Thank goodness Hudson is such a good sleeper—almost too good. I have to run his legs under cold water to wake him up to eat. I don't stress about this. I hardly stress about anything now that he's here. All of the anxiety and depression I experienced while pregnant has evaporated now that Hudson is with me. He and I go to the mall, and to the movies, and for long walks around Coto de Caza.

I love being with him. It feels like what I was meant to do all along.

FORTY-THREE

I FLY TO UTAH TO SIGN THE PAPERWORK TO GO BACK TO school. Hudson comes with me. He's only four weeks old but behaves perfectly on the plane. He behaves perfectly everywhere: sleeping, nestling against my chest, practicing tummy time on the floor.

Still, it's hard for me to be back in Utah. Everything reminds me of Arik: it's like visiting for his funeral all over again. I wonder if I'll ever walk around BYU and not see him smiling at me from under his blue hat, or hear his laugh at Legends Grille.

My first full day in town, Lauren and I go to BYU to meet with advisors and administrators to discuss my return to tennis. I'm excited to get back on the court, but it feels weird to talk about playing because I'm not technically even cleared to work out yet. My incision is getting better. I don't have any gauze inside the wound anymore. But it's still painful to sneeze and laugh. I can't imagine jumping or hitting a ball.

That night, Lauren has the tennis team over to her house. Two recruits are visiting, and the team is planning to go out afterward. I tell them I'm not going to go, but eventually everyone—including Lauren—convinces me to throw together a costume. It's Halloween weekend: the same weekend I visited as a seventeen-year-old. It's so weird to be in the same place and feel so different.

I don't feel ready to go to a party. I'm insecure about my body and my new status as a single mom, but I draw some whiskers on my cheeks, put some cat ears over my side part, and go out with the team. It's the first time I've ever left Hudson.

The second we get to the party, which is at the Startup Building in Provo, my boobs fill with milk. It's incredibly uncomfortable. They feel like they're going to explode. I go inside and try to ignore the pain, but I feel incredibly out of place. I've been to this type of party a million times—DJ, strobe lights, dancing—but I feel awkward and foreign and sad. I can't shake the feeling that I don't belong here anymore and that everyone else can tell. It doesn't help that someone recognizes me and yells, "Mayci? What are you doing here? Didn't you just have a baby?" I'm relieved to go back to Lauren's house and see Hudson. For so long, having him inside me made me feel out of place and lonely, but now, I feel most at home when I'm with him.

COLE AND I HAVE been texting since before I had Hudson. He knows I'm visiting Utah for the week and wants to meet up. The last time I saw him, he told me not to make bad choices. Now I have a baby, I've been assaulted, and I've gone through a phase of heavy drinking—all the things he'd warned me not to do that day at the beach.

I don't know what it will be like to see him. I'm not sure I'm ready. But I make plans to meet him at a party I'm going to with Amy and her fiancé.

I dress up as a basketball player, mostly so I won't have to wear anything form-fitting. I'm too insecure about the baby weight.

I recognize Cole the second he walks into the party. His walk is so familiar.

The party is bad, and we leave after a couple minutes, driving to Walmart for Red Bull and trying to decide where to go next. Amy and her fiancé want to go home. Cole asks me if I want to try a different dance party. The curious part of me is tempted to go with him, but I know I need to go back to Lauren and Kirk's. I'm afraid of what'll happen if Cole and I stay out later. I don't trust this new version of myself. I don't entirely know who she is. And I'm afraid of dancing with Cole. I'm self-conscious that he'll feel the baby weight on me, or worse, try to kiss me. I'm nowhere near ready for that. I like Cole.

I see him as a good friend. But Arik just died. I can't start anything new right now, and I don't want to.

I tell Cole I have to get back to my son, and he drives me the twenty minutes to Lauren and Kirk's. I thank him, get out of his car, and tiptoe up the stairs and into the room where Hudson is sleeping soundly in his crib. I stand over him and watch his tiny chest rise and fall. I exhale. I'm safe again.

FORTY-FOUR

I'M CLEARED TO WORK OUT. IT'S NOVEMBER. I HAVE FIVE weeks to get in shape before tennis season starts. I haven't played in almost nine months. I haven't run or jumped or worked on my serve. The scar from my C-section is still pink and raised. But it's time.

My dad hires a personal trainer named Josh to work with me on speed, strength, and overall conditioning. He's in his thirties and always wears a hat. The first day I meet with him, his warm-up takes me an hour, but I don't feel discouraged. I'm excited to get back in shape. I'm excited for my body to do more than feed Hudson eight times a day.

With Josh I do bear crawls, push-ups, battle ropes, and planks. My abs, which completely separated to grow Hudson, and which were pulled apart by the surgeon when I delivered him, start to come back online. After the first session, I can barely feel them. But after a second and third, they tingle, which reminds me that they're there. Eventually, I understand they're working again.

I stop breastfeeding. I'd never set out to do it in the first place, and while I was surprised to discover I liked it, it's too hard to get back in tennis shape and feed Hudson at the same time. I feel fine about stopping. I'm proud of myself for doing it at all.

I PLAY TENNIS FOR the first time. My mom takes me out to the courts near our house and we hit together. We play easy. There's no running for balls. No serving. Definitely no lunging. I feel rusty, but I'm happy to be moving.

On the drive back to our house, we don't talk about the significance of me playing tennis again. We act like it's a completely normal day, even though Hudson's been with us the whole time.

We play again the next morning, and the morning after that. My game starts to come back. Or at least, most of it does. My forehand, which has always been my strength, feels different. There's something wrong with it. I can't figure it out. The ball, which I've always hit a certain way, doesn't respond how I expect it to. I try changing my grip, but that doesn't work. I'm someone who relies heavily on feel while playing tennis: the feel of the grip, of the ball, of my shoes. I can't feel my forehand anymore.

My parents hire my high school coach, Chris, who's from New Zealand and used to be a pro, to help me. I like Chris. Everyone does. After one of our lessons, he meets me at the net and says, "It's weird that you could take this much time off and be just as good." That's as close as we ever get to talking about Hudson.

Driving home, I run a hand along my C-section scar. I think about what would've happened to my tennis career if I hadn't met Dick, if I hadn't slept with Arik, if I hadn't let myself get so distracted by parties and boys. My parents used to say I had "the curse of the talented." They meant I was gifted enough to not apply myself. I didn't believe them. Now, turning onto my parents' street, I wish I'd worked harder. I know I'm not going to be a pro tennis player anymore. But I also know if I focus, I can get back to playing number one at BYU.

I try to eat better. No more 44-ounce Polar Pops filled with Dr Pepper. No more endless pizza. Maybe even a vegetable or two. I want to take better care of myself than I did freshman and sophomore years, when I subsisted on vodka, doughnuts, and Swig. That doesn't mean I'm going to give up doughnuts. But I'm done drinking. And I'm done with sex before marriage.

TOLD YOU SO

All these bad things have happened to me because of the poor decisions I've made. I'm ready to follow the church's guidelines. I'm ready to be a good Mormon. After years of mistakes, I finally understand the reasoning behind the church's rules. But I still don't think people should be shamed for bending them.

FORTY-FIVE

AMY GETS MARRIED IN UTAH. IT'S DECEMBER, AND HUDson sees snow for the first time. My mom, who comes with me, watches him so I can perform my maid-of-honor duties. I wear a gold sequin dress with Spanx. During the wedding, I don't even think about being single, or missing Arik, or the fact that in another life I would've been married already. I'm too focused on Amy, which is how it should be.

A couple days later, my mom, Hudson, and I fly back to California to prepare for me to go to school.

The plan is for me, Hudson, and my mom to move in with Lauren, Kirk, and Presley in Vineyard. They have two extra bedrooms. We'll all live together while I go back to BYU. There's not even a question of whether my mom will come with me. I don't think we even talk about it. She and my dad have always supported my tennis: they've flown to almost all of my matches, in Arizona and Virginia and Oregon. Somehow it doesn't seem so different for my mom to sacrifice her life in California and move to Utah with me, even if it means she and my dad will now be living in different states.

IT NORMALLY TAKES TEN hours to drive to Utah. But Hudson needs a bottle and a diaper change every two hours, so we end up spending the night in Saint George and getting to Lauren and Kirk's house a day later than we expected. I'm so grateful my mom's with me. And that Lauren and Kirk have let us move in. It's not easy to have someone living in your house, eating your food, and raising their kid in your space. But Lauren and Kirk are amazing about it. Lauren's the oldest sibling in our family, and it's almost innate for her to take the rest of us in. Both McCall and Alex have lived with her already.

Living together makes the two of us even closer. We get lunch on campus, and hang out after practice, and watch our babies play together.

Hudson and Presley are only a year and a half apart, so it starts to feel like they're siblings. When I get home from practice, we put on music and have dance parties with the babies in the living room. On Sunday nights, we make grilled chicken and salad and hang out as a family. Kirk basically becomes Hudson's surrogate dad.

I MISS HUDSON WHEN I'm at school. I have a heavy course load and three hours of tennis practice a day. A 1.9 (or even a 2.4) GPA isn't going to cut it for me now that I'm a single mom. I know I need to study and get a degree I can use so that I can get a good job to support my son.

Some days, I have night classes and don't get home until after my mom has put Hudson to bed. I peek in on him sleeping in his crib. I watch his chest rise and fall, a pacifier covering half his face, and wonder how it's possible to love someone so much.

Other nights, my mom keeps Hudson awake so I can see him. I'll play with him for an hour, put him to bed, then do my homework. I won't get to sleep until two a.m.

My mom never complains about taking care of Hudson. I only learn how hard it was for her years later, when my dad tells me she called, two days after we moved into Lauren's house, to say she couldn't do it. She couldn't take care of Hudson twelve hours a day. But she did.

TOLD YOU SO

MY FIRST MATCH IS in Virginia. Hudson is three and a half months old. My whole family decides to come. At the Salt Lake City airport, Delta has signs welcoming BYU tennis to our flight. Before I had Hudson, seeing these always made me feel so excited. Now, with my tennis bag on one shoulder and Hudson's diaper bag on the other, I'm anxious—painfully aware of the fact that BYU tennis has an entire Jones family entourage.

In some ways, it's always been like this. When it didn't make sense for Lauren to take maternity leave, my mom became Presley's fly-along nanny. She's doing the same thing for me now, just paying for her own ticket. But there's something about this that feels different. Maybe it's because I didn't do preseason with the team because I was recovering from having a baby. Or maybe it's because Lauren is pregnant again. Whatever the reason, I never felt so stuck between my family and my tennis team before; somehow, subtly, it feels like the Joneses and BYU tennis are on opposite sides, which is weird, because the Joneses *are* BYU tennis.

I try to ignore this. But it's hard. Since I've come back to school, there have been whispers on the team that I shouldn't be playing number one, that I'm only in that spot because Lauren's my sister. I've beaten all the other girls at practice. I've earned my spot back. But my teammates haven't welcomed me back the way I'd hoped they would. Even Lauren's boss has warned her about playing me in the top spot. He's told her to be careful that it doesn't look like she's favoring me. "I'm not favoring her," Lauren tells him in a meeting. "She's the best."

I know that's true. But I have to prove it in season too. And for the first time, I feel this guilt and anxiety about it that I haven't experienced before.

IT'S SNOWING IN VIRGINIA when we land. Charlottesville, where we're playing four teams as part of an early-season pod, isn't equipped to handle the weather. They don't even have enough snowplows. The drive to our hotel is sketchy, but I feel invincible. I've gone through so much I feel like God isn't going to screw with me. It's almost like I have a free pass.

We get settled at our hotel. Hudson is an easy baby, but no baby, no matter how easy, is happy after a cross-country flight and a long drive. Lauren goes to the grocery store to get snacks. It's impossible for us to go to a team dinner because the roads are so bad.

She comes back with water bottles, Power Bars, and Gatorade. No bread, because other people have bought it all in a panic. It's like Charlottesville is preparing for the apocalypse.

I'm so grateful for my mom, who makes it all feel fun. I know Hudson is safe with her. I can hydrate, eat, and get ready for my match.

And I'm grateful for Taylah, who I'm rooming with on this trip. She's a freshman on the team from Australia. Lauren told me she would be a good friend for me, and she's right. Taylah is tall, quiet, and kind. She doesn't make me feel weird for having a baby. She acts like it's normal, and we become friends right away.

The day of the match, I play Danielle Collins, who's a pro now. It's my official return to collegiate tennis after having a baby. I'm only a few months postpartum. Danielle, on the other hand, has just won NCAAs.

I lose, but I put up a good fight and make her work for it. I'm proud of myself until I hear what some of my teammates are saying behind my back. They're saying I don't deserve to be number one, that Tara does, that Lauren played me in the top spot because of nepotism. And they're saying I cheated the BYU honor code to get back into school, which is funny because most of the girls saying that don't follow the honor code at all.

I'm devastated and angry. Nothing I've done—from meeting with the awful bishop once a week to taking all those classes while mourning Arik to sticking a Q-Tip one inch into my infected abdomen—has been remotely easy or fun. I've earned my ecclesiastical endorsement. I've repented. Nobody in my family has cheated. We've done everything by the book. I can't believe some of my teammates and best friends aren't supporting me after I had my baby so recently. It breaks my heart.

TENNIS IS A MENTAL game as much as a physical one. I don't play as well when I know people are talking about me behind my back. At practice,

I'm distracted. And during matches, I feel an added pressure to win to prove some of my teammates wrong. I still have no idea what I did to make them upset. I ask them to hang out or talk.

Tara says, "You're a mom now."

I don't know what that means. Are moms not supposed to have friends?

I'M STARTING TO FEEL micromanaged at Lauren's house too. It's nobody's fault. Lauren is pregnant, which is hard under the best circumstances, and the team drama is affecting her too. As head coach, she's responsible for her players on and off the court. Half the girls are on our side and half the girls are on Tara, Nicole, and Amy's side. Lauren's assistant coach is doing her best, but she can't seem to straddle the divide.

Meanwhile, my mom's worried I'm going to start partying again. I'll be hanging out with people and say, "OK, I have to go home now," and they'll joke about me having a curfew and I'll be like, "No, actually yes. I literally do." It's like I'm in high school again.

Sometimes, my mom flies back to California to visit my dad. If I have a lot going on at school or with tennis, she'll take Hudson with her.

When she does this, she tracks my location to make sure I keep curfew. I've lost three of my closest friends: Tara and I were inseparable. Nicole and I have known each other since we were twelve. I was the maid of honor at Amy's wedding. Without them and without Arik, I start to feel like I've lost everyone. I lie in bed, missing my son and missing my friends and missing Arik. I try to battle the depression that I can feel coming back.

FORTY-SIX

I'M IN MY BEDROOM WHEN MY PHONE RINGS. I'M EXPECTING a call, so I pick up. The person on the other line says, "Mayci?" It's like he knows me. Except he doesn't. His name is Dan, and he says he thinks I'm cute. He tells me he saw me play tennis and can't stop thinking about me. I ask how he got my number.

He says, "I'm a renaissance man. I have my ways."

I don't know if I should hang up or keep talking to him. I'm both freaked out and flattered, and after a few minutes, I realize I'm still on the phone with him.

I find Dan engaging. And I'm lonely.

Cole and I are still hanging out, but infrequently. I don't know how to date after Arik. I feel a little like "used goods." I don't know why anyone would be interested in me. I've lost all of my confidence. While other college students are living near campus and going out every night, I'm standing in line at the grocery store trying to calm a crying Hudson while the cashier types in the code from my food stamp voucher. I get them through the Utah Woman, Infants and Children program. Formula and solids are expensive, and even though my family helps so much with housing and childcare, they're not paying for everything. WIC is helpful. But it's a complicated and embarrassing system. Each month, I get a check that needs to be used for specific things:

- 1 (16 oz) cheese—string or block. No slices.
- 4 (15 to 16 oz size) approved canned beans
- 1 (gallon) cow's milk—whole fat

Everything is so specific. It literally takes fifteen minutes to check out.

THE FIRST ANNIVERSARY OF Arik's death is a struggle. All of March feels gloomy. At a pre-match practice in Washington, Lauren asks if I'm OK. I'm obviously not. I start crying. I miss Arik so much.

The next day, I'm playing on the number one court when Tara loses her match and starts shouting at Lauren, who's twenty weeks pregnant. There are matches happening on the other courts. Everyone stops playing and stares at Tara and Lauren.

From the sideline, I can see Lauren's expression. She looks embarrassed and shocked, her face flushed, one hand on her baby bump.

Afterward, we go out to team dinner. Someone writes "NEPOTISM" on the paper tablecloth. I can tell Lauren is uncomfortable. She's always calm, always collected. But she's quiet the rest of the meal. The word on the table is staring at all of us.

Later, Lauren calls her boss at BYU—the one who'd told her to be careful about playing me at number one. He says Lauren can't cut Tara from the team. He's a mellow guy. Passive. He tells Lauren to "just try to talk to her."

Lauren does, and later I hear that Tara may have recorded the conversation, then edited the audio so it seemed like Lauren was shit-talking other players. Tara has always been Lauren's favorite—Lauren has literally said that to me—so it's ironic that it seems like Tara is now trying to get Lauren fired.

ALL SEASON, I'VE BEEN playing doubles with Tara. But when Lauren gets an email from someone who saw our team at the airport and overheard Tara make some disturbing comments about punching her, she decides it's time to change the lineup, and she pairs me with Taylah.

Taylah and I play well together and win a lot of our matches. It's fun, and we become even closer. She gets me to start going out again and reminds me that I can still have a social life, even though I'm a mom and three of my best friends have basically started to hate me overnight.

As I get my confidence back, I continue talking to Dan. One day, when I'm sitting at my desk in Lauren and Kirk's house, I ask him if he has social media. I want to know what he looks like. He's been talking about taking me on a date. He says we're going to go indoor skydiving, which sounds fun.

"I don't have social media," he says.

I decide to look him up. All along, I'd assumed he was my age, but when I find his photo on his company's website, he looks like he could be friends with my dad. He's bald and his beard is graying. I feel grossed out that he's so much older than me. I ghost him. But he keeps texting me. I start to worry he's going to show up at one of my matches because the schedule is online. I text him and tell him I have a boyfriend, just to get him to stop talking to me. It doesn't work. I hear from him again and again. He asks how I'm doing. He tells me he's rich. He talks a lot about how he owns his company and has a private plane. I'm like, *You know what? I don't need that if it comes with you. Leave me alone.*

I'M SCANNING THE STANDS, looking for Dan, when I hear screaming. I look over at Tara, who's playing a match one court over. She's acting erratic—shouting each time she wins a point and egging on the crowd. BYU's vice president is watching. And other people are yelling now too. Amy's husband, who's in the stands, is shouting, "Yeah, Tara! That's how a real number one player plays." It feels like some of my teammates are even rooting for my opponent. It's like they want me to lose. It's a knife to the heart. I win my first set, but don't get to finish the match because our team loses while I'm still playing. It's disappointing. I wanted to finish and show everyone I could do it. But part of me feels so sad and guilty about playing number one that I want to be moved down in the lineup. Maybe then I could get my friends back.

Afterward, Lauren's boss tells her that Tara shouldn't be on the team anymore. Lauren helps Tara figure out the transfer portal. When other coaches call to ask about her, Lauren doesn't say anything negative.

I'm glad Tara gets settled somewhere else, but sad to never get closure with her. After she leaves BYU, I text her saying that I'm sorry if I hurt her. I ask if I did something to make her upset. I never learn why she was so mad at me, even when I follow up. It breaks my heart to lose her as a friend.

Tara loved Arik. They were close. Losing her is almost like another severed cord.

FORTY-SEVEN

I'M AT A PARTY WITH TAYLAH. IT'S LAME, AND WE'RE GETting ready to leave. I have to get home to make my curfew. We go out to my car, where Taylah says she's not ready to turn in for the night. She wants to find an afterparty. I wait in the car while she goes back inside to see if there's anything good happening in Provo.

When she comes back out to the car, she's excited about a bonfire happening at a guy named Jacob's house. She tells me about it while I drive her back to her dorm. I tell her to have fun, then head back to Lauren's house, where my mom and Hudson are both asleep.

The next morning at tennis practice, Taylah's energetic. Giddy, even. Which is surprising since she's been up all night. She tells me, "I met the hottest guy."

She explains that she never kisses guys the first day she meets them, but that Jacob told her it was technically the next day, and that they made out after the cops shut down the fifty-person bonfire in his backyard.

Jacob is working a sales party later. He invites Taylah, who wants me to come meet him. She needs a wing-woman because she can be shy, especially around new guys. My mom is happy to watch Hudson, so Taylah and I go.

When I walk in and see Jacob, the first thing I think is that Taylah wasn't exaggerating: he's hot. He's tan and tall and wearing a black leather jacket. We talk about Southern California, and the places we know in common.

The whole time I wonder how Taylah managed to find a guy in Utah who's attractive, from Southern California, *and* Mormon. I don't think about trying to steal him from her. I would never do that. But I can't help but notice how intrigued I am by him, and after I leave the party, I call my parents and tell them that Taylah's just met the hottest guy from California. They look at his Instagram.

"Yeah," my dad says, on the phone. "He's a good-looking dude."

I KNOW JACOB HAS a past. I have a sixth sense about these things. I can always tell, when I meet a Mormon guy, if he's a virgin, if he drinks, if he used to drink, if he's running away from something. Later, I'll learn that Jacob grew up with people who mostly weren't Mormon, and that he smoked, drank, and had sex when he was in high school.

Jacob and Taylah hang out for the rest of the semester, which is only three weeks. I spend time with them too. The three of us go on a double date with Cole, who I'm still casually seeing. We meet at a random parking lot at BYU. Everyone gets in my car. Jacob wants to set off a firework, so we drive up to a viewing area.

When we get there, Jacob and Taylah set the firework off while Cole and I sit in the car and talk. He tells me how much he likes me and that he thought about me when he was on mission. I nod and think about how I want to switch dates with Taylah. I know I'm not into Cole anymore. I'm glad we reconnected. He was my first kiss after Arik—a little more than one year after Arik's death. But I get the vibe that he's not interested in being a dad anytime soon, and I just don't have the spark with him. I only see him as a friend, so I know things will fizzle out soon.

When Taylah and Jacob get back in the car, I drive the four of us down the hill, where I drop off Taylah and Cole first, then spend ten minutes in the car alone with Jacob en route to dropping him off at his place. He moves to the front seat. We don't flirt. I know he's not in school, and he knows I have a kid—that things are messy for me. But there's a vibe. We can both feel it.

TOLD YOU SO

I GET JACOB'S NUMBER because I want to throw Taylah a birthday party. I tell Jacob to blow off Taylah that night, to pretend like he's not going to see her. She gets upset. Jacob's leaving for California the next day. She wanted to say bye.

When he jumps out from behind a couch at our teammate Sarah's parents' house, she beams. We play water pong and listen to music in the basement.

At the end of the night, we watch a movie: me, Jacob, Taylah, Sarah, her boyfriend Derek, and Sarah's friend Joe, who's my date. Sarah set me up with him because things with Cole are finally almost done. We're still talking, but he's seeing other people, and I want to be too.

Joe and I make out on one end of the couch while Jacob and Taylah kiss on the other. On the floor, Sarah and Derek are kissing. Joe is my second kiss since Arik. Kissing Cole had felt totally normal, because we'd done it before. This is different. There's no real connection between us, but it's exciting to be kissing someone new after feeling sad for so long. It's taken thirteen months, but I feel like I'm slowly getting out of the grief stage. I feel like my confidence is slowly coming back. I'm beginning to move on.

FORTY-EIGHT

IN THE SPRING, I GET AN INTERNSHIP AT ABC NEWS IN UTAH. I go three days a week, starting at seven a.m. I don't want to do hard news—it's too depressing. It's always about the worst, most traumatic story. I'll never forget the way networks reported on Arik's death as if he weren't a real person. I want to do something kinder. Stories that make people feel warm and optimistic. I work on a talk show called *Good Things Utah*.

It's my first taste of broadcast journalism. There are cooking segments, tidbits of celebrity gossip, and fun stories about events happening around Utah. My job is to take behind-the-scenes photos, do the dishes after the cooking segments, greet guests and escort them to their segments, and schedule posts to go up on Facebook, which is the only social media we use. I hate using the copy machine. It stresses me out. But I like the rest of the work, especially coming up with ideas for segments and scheduling social media content that aligns with the show.

I don't know this yet, but it's good practice.

One morning, I'm standing behind a camera and talking to a guest. I mention that I have a kid out of wedlock. I'm self-conscious about the fact that I don't have a wedding ring, so I usually preempt any questions or judgment. I hate the idea of someone asking, "Where's your husband?" I don't want to deal with that.

The guest looks at me from the stage and says, "You know, you don't have to say that. You don't owe anyone an explanation."

I've never thought of it that way before. It builds my confidence.

So do my grades for the semester, which are good. I get a 4.0. I'm proud that I did well in all my classes. Looking at my transcript, I think it's insane that there was a time when I didn't want a career. Why would I want to go to school and not use my degree? I begin to realize that Arik's passing and Hudson's birth have been a wakeup call. I understand, now, that life won't be easy. It's up to me to make things happen. I can feel myself becoming more motivated and driven—and more interesting. I start to like myself. I appreciate who I'm becoming for the first time in years.

I go home for the summer. Jacob is in Southern California too. He's selling pest control and living in Rancho Mission Viejo, which is ten minutes from my parents' house. Going door-to-door is hard work. Jacob knocks six days a week, all day long. It's how he'll end up paying for college.

After a month, I decide to reach out to him to hang out as friends. I ask Taylah if it's OK first, and she says of course. She's back home in Australia.

I don't text Jacob in a flirty way. I just want friends back home, since most of mine haven't come back from college for the summer. And I like spending time with him.

He comes over to my parents' house a few days later. He brings some of the guys he works with, and we all hot-tub. It's late—Hudson's already gone to sleep. I don't want him to grow up wondering why there are random guys around.

But Jacob starts coming by more and more, until he's regularly hot-tubbing with me four evenings a week. My parents love him.

One afternoon, when my mom and I are standing in the kitchen together, my mom tells me to look at his lips. "Don't you want to kiss them?" she asks.

"He was seeing Taylah last semester," I tell her. "So, no."

But I find myself looking at Jacob's lips even more often. When Dan, the old guy, texts me, I say I'm really serious with my boyfriend. What I mean is that I have a crush on Jacob, even though I know I shouldn't. Jacob and Taylah never officially dated. They're not even in touch now. But I don't want to hurt our friendship.

TOLD YOU SO

ONE NIGHT, WHEN I'M at dinner with McCall and her family, Jacob texts asking what I'm up to. I've never let him see Hudson, so when I respond saying I'm at dinner with him, I assume Jacob knows that that means we can't hang out.

Instead, he responds, "Oh, good. I've been wanting to meet Hudson."

I panic. I'm not ready for Hudson to meet a guy I have a crush on.

But when Jacob gets to the restaurant, which is casual, he's immediately sweet with Hudson, cuddling with him and making him laugh.

I'm not happy about it at all. It makes my crush worse, and I'm worried Hudson will get attached.

After dinner, Jacob comes back to my parents' house. I change Hudson into his pajamas—blue footies—then ask Jacob to watch him for a minute while I run upstairs.

When I come back down, they're playing together. Hudson is laughing. Jacob's on his hands and knees on the carpet.

I watch for a moment, half-hidden behind the wall. I can't tell if Jacob likes me. He never flirts with me. But I know I like him a lot. And I know, finally, that I have my confidence back. That I can still be someone's dream girl.

"Hey," I say, stepping toward Hudson and Jacob. "Everything good?"

"Everything's great," Jacob says, smiling.

FORTY-NINE

TAYLAH TEXTS ME: "THIS IS RANDOM, BUT I THINK YOU and Jacob would actually be a really cute couple." It's a relief to have her support. But Jacob and I are firmly in the friend zone. When we meet for lunch during his long days, we never flirt. And when we hang out together after his shifts, everything is chill. I'm nervous to change that and step out of the friend zone, but the next time he comes over and we hot-tub together, I decide to flirt with him and see how it's received. I tell him he's not a fun texter.

"What do you mean?" he asks, splashing the water.

"You never flirt," I say, looking at him. "You're not fun."

Jacob grabs me and pulls me onto his lap in the hot tub. I get nervous. This is the first time I've had a big crush on someone since having Hudson. What if Jacob hurts me? What if we ruin our friendship? I look at him, and we kiss. Afterward, we're both grinning, but I don't know if it's the start of something serious or a one-time thing.

IT'S THE START OF something serious. Jacob and I never have a conversation about the fact that we're not going to have sex. I know he's on a good path because he's talking about going on mission. And he knows that everything after Arik died was so horrible that I never want to be pregnant and single again.

It's nice to be with someone who understands where I'm coming from—someone who's also trying to be a little more spiritual.

In August, Hudson takes his first steps out of Jacob's arms. It's almost bedtime. Jacob's been knocking doors all day. He's still wearing his uniform: khaki shorts and a blue polo. Hudson is in his pajamas. He toddles toward me and I beam.

At the end of the summer, Jacob volunteers to drive back to Utah with me, my mom, and Hudson. He sits in the back seat with Hudson the whole way, entertaining him for the entire ten-hour drive. It's clear he's special. Everyone loves him. But I'm not ready to settle down yet. I'm terrified of getting hurt. And Jacob isn't perfectly on track with his life. Don't get me wrong: he's not a mess. He's been supporting himself financially since he graduated high school. But he's not enrolled in a four-year college, and I know I want any guy I date to be pursuing a bachelor's degree.

DURING THE FALL SEMESTER, Jacob goes to Japan for a month and we message every day. We're not dating, but when it's four p.m. in Utah and eight a.m. in Tokyo, I text Jacob telling him that I want to FaceTime. We go back and forth about when we'll both have Wi-Fi.

Later, when we're texting again, he tells me I need to read *The Continuous Atonement*. I call it a church book but say it looks good. I tell him about reading *The Miracle of Forgiveness*. I say it's good and scary.

When Jacob asks me why it's scary, I explain that it made me feel like a bad person because it argues that sex is considered a sin just behind killing someone.

He writes back, "I'm not sure I wanna read that then," with the slanted-face emoji.

He tells me he wants to speak in church, which is what we call it when someone in church leadership gives you a topic to talk about in front of the whole congregation. I make fun of him for being motivated, but I'm proud of him. We bond over the fact that we're both bad at expressing our emotions. I text him, "I have a hard time telling my parents/friends or anyone that I even like someone." I add a "haha," and then, "I have issues." I explain that sometimes I'll get pissed and bottle up my anger until it explodes. I worry that sounds weird, but he tells me that's normal. He says he can be closed off from his family too.

FIFTY

I TEXT JACOB EVERY DAY THAT HE'S GONE, BUT I TEXT OTHER guys too. BYU in the fall is made for dating, and I refuse to be tied down. Hudson isn't even a year old.

I'm walking to the Student Athlete Building when I see Liam. I haven't talked to him since he told me he couldn't come over to Lauren's house for dinner and I chose Arik. I feel shy now, embarrassed. So much has happened since then.

But when we make eye contact, I say hi.

"Do you remember me?" I ask.

"Of course I remember you," he says.

I give him my number, then go to my tennis workout. By the time I'm finished, he's texted asking me to hang out. I respond, "Yes." I feel totally giddy. This is the guy I told my parents I was going to marry. I feel like it might still be true.

My mom has a rule that I have to stop by Lauren's to put Hudson to sleep every night before going back out. She wants me to have time with him every day, and I want that too.

I drive the twenty minutes to the house in Vineyard, where I give Hudson a bottle and read him a book, then drive back to Provo, where I go to Liam's apartment.

We talk for three hours. I never mention my son. My heart starts racing each time I think about bringing Hudson up. I don't want to be judged, and I want to protect Hudson.

I HANG OUT WITH Liam again, and with a guy named Zack. It feels good to have my confidence back, to no longer be actively grieving or feuding with my old teammates.

When Liam and I go to his apartment again, I tell him I have a baby, and he says he knows. Some of the guys on the football team told him. It doesn't bother him. He thinks it's cool.

Jacob is still in Japan. I'm excited for him to come back to Utah, but he's still planning to go on mission, so it's not like we can be anything serious anyway.

And our lives are so different. I'm living with my son, my mom, my sister, her husband, and their kids. Jacob has fifteen roommates in this Mormon frat house overlooking BYU. The first time I went over there, a bunch of guys were dipping pieces of Wonder bread in water and slapping each other in the face with them. Jacob didn't participate, but it still gave me a major ick. I'm a mom, for heaven's sake.

Still, I'm thrilled to see Jacob when he's back. He picks me up at the airport because I'm returning from a tennis trip. He brings bagels and we walk around the capitol in Salt Lake City. It's always weird to finally see someone you've been texting for a month in person, but it also feels natural—like we've known each other for longer than six months.

TWO WEEKS AFTER JACOB gets back from Japan, when we're sitting in his car outside Lauren's house, he turns to me and asks to define our relationship. He wants to be my boyfriend. I tell him I need to think about it. I'm having fun being single. Taylah and I go out together and gossip about the boys we're seeing. And while I really like Jacob, he's a year younger than me and in such a different life stage. I just don't think it'll work.

I have this feeling that the next person I seriously date, I'm going to marry. I can't marry someone who's about to spend two years abroad on a mission.

Plus, I still find Liam so hot.

I start ignoring Jacob's texts, but he doesn't take it personally. When I do respond, he jumps at the chance to hang out. He comes over and helps make dinner for me, Lauren, Kirk, and my mom, or to play with Hudson.

Sometimes, when I ghost him for a while, he'll text my mom, who loves him. She'll even invite him over herself when I make up excuses not to see him.

Over Thanksgiving, when we're both in California visiting our families, we go watch a sunset from the cliffs in San Diego. I'm terrified he's going to tell me he loves me. He just has this look on his face.

WHEN I GET BACK to campus, I talk to Taylah about Jacob. We're at her apartment getting ready to go out. She's putting on makeup, her brown hair loosely curled. I'm sitting on the bed.

I tell Taylah that I really like Jacob, that I'm thinking about agreeing to officially date him. She convinces me not to. We're both having so much fun being single together. Why would I settle down early? Why not enjoy being in college for a little while longer? After all, I'm only twenty-one.

I ghost Jacob for the second time. I keep seeing Liam and Zack. But Jacob is the best. He drops off my favorite breakfast one morning before I fly to San Francisco for a preseason match: Kneaders French toast, OJ, and a side of fruit he leaves on Lauren and Kirk's front porch.

A month later, in December, I decide it's time to give him a shot. Nothing's changed. He's still planning to go on mission. He's still younger than me, and he's still living with fifteen men who like to slap each other in the face with wet Wonder bread. I'm still not ready to be tied down. But he's just too amazing. I know if I don't give him a real chance, I'll always regret it. He could be my person. He could be Hudson's dad. He already acts like it.

FIFTY-ONE

I'M SITTING AT A RESTAURANT IN NEWPORT BEACH. IT'S MY mom's birthday. Hudson, who's fourteen months old, is in a high chair beside me. He's acting wild: shrieking and throwing forks on the floor. It's mostly cute, but a little loud, and when our food comes, a lady walks up to our table. "I hope you've enjoyed your dinner," she says. I look up and smile, about to thank her, when she says, "Because you have certainly ruined mine."

I glance at my parents, glad they haven't heard. I'm embarrassed and confused.

Parenting is easier in Utah. There are more kids around, and people are generally nicer. I'm happy to leave Orange County and drive home with Jacob, Hudson, and my mom a couple days later. The winter tennis season is starting. I have a feeling this is going to be my year. For once, I'm not coming back from anything.

MY FIRST MATCH IS against Weber. I stand on the court and look for Jacob. We've just started seriously dating, and he's promised me he's going to be there. My parents are in the stands, and his are supposed to come too. It'll be the first time they meet.

Except yesterday Jacob decided to go to Vegas to celebrate a few guys' birthdays for the night in an old, short school bus that barely works. Before he left, I told him it was a bad plan. And what do you know, the bus broke down somewhere in Nevada. Now he's trying to hitchhike back to campus to make it to the match in time.

I run a hand down my racket and glance up at the stands again. Liz, Arik's mom, is there too. I wave to her. I don't care how Jacob gets from the middle of nowhere to Provo, I just care that he does. I know my worth now. I want a partner who's going to show up for the things that are important to me. Jacob needs to be at my opening match senior year, or I'll know where his real priorities lie. I'm not going to settle. It's not an option.

JACOB GETS TO CAMPUS forty minutes after I start playing. I win, because I always win against Weber. His parents spend the match with mine. Afterward, we all go to California Pizza Kitchen. Jacob holds my hand under the table.

I want to go to sleep, but Jacob needs to go and get his backpack, which he'd left on the broken-down bus. He's worried it's going to get stolen if it stays there overnight. I go with him.

In the car, he looks at me and says, "There were all these girls on the Vegas trip, and I didn't even care about them. It made me realize that the only person I have eyes for is you. I love you."

I stare at him like, *Excuse me? That's how you're going to tell me you love me? By mentioning other girls?*

But twenty minutes later I tell him, "I love you too."

It's the first time I've said it since Arik. I feel scared but sure.

LATER, JACOB TELLS ME he's prayed and decided he isn't going to go on mission after all. His mission is something else: to raise a family with me. I'm relieved, but I also knew he would say this the second we started officially dating. I hope his family's OK with it. And I hope there isn't a pressure to get married. I'm still not ready. I'm having too much fun. I still have my curfew, so I get an iPad and tie my location to that. When my mom's in California, I drop the iPad off at my sister's house and go out with Jacob and Taylah. I don't feel bad about it. If I were drinking or partying again, it would be a problem. But I'm not. I'm just out having a good time.

FIFTY-TWO

I PLAY ANOTHER TENNIS MATCH. IT'S FEBRUARY NOW, almost a year and a half since I had Hudson. There's no drama on the team anymore, so I can focus. And my body finally feels legible to me again. Strong. My forehand is back after struggling with it last year.

I'm playing a girl I lost to the year before, but this time I'm winning.

I'm wearing new shoes. BYU gives them to us all the time, but I prefer to play in old tennis shoes. I use them until I'm sliding all over the indoor courts. These new ones are too sticky. My opponent hits a lob while I'm at the net. It goes over my head. I run to the baseline and plant my foot, but I've stopped a little too short. I have to reach my body and twist. My foot doesn't move with me. My knee collapses in on itself. I hear a pop.

I can't bend or straighten my knee. I hop on my good leg, then lower myself onto the court until I'm lying down. Everyone watching is like, *What the heck?* Nobody comes to check on me for a full two minutes because I don't cry or yell.

When the trainer finally comes over, I tear up. My knee hurts. The trainer helps me walk back to the bench. Lauren, who's been on another court, walks over. She asks what's going on.

I tell her, "I hurt my knee."

The trainer is looking at it.

He says, "Mayci shouldn't play anymore."

Lauren says, "What do you mean?"

The trainer almost always lets injured players on the court. He's very "tough love." He doesn't really believe in sitting things out.

"Why don't you try walking to the fence and back?" Lauren asks.

I stand and walk to the fence. I feel a little better. The adrenaline is kicking in.

"Jog now," the trainer says. I do. It feels fine. I'm relieved. I know how to play injured. I've gone onto the court after pulling muscles, after having food poisoning, after getting the flu. I've literally gotten IVs from BYU Athletics to get me back out there. "Move your leg side to side."

I do and my leg collapses. You can see the joints look wrong.

The trainer looks at Lauren and says, "She can't play."

Lauren says, "Are you sure?"

The trainer nods. I have to forfeit the match.

He puts me on crutches and sends one of the assistant trainers to help me get my stuff from the locker room. While I'm changing, the trainer tells my parents he thinks I tore my ACL. My parents are shocked. The Joneses have ankle issues, not knee ones.

I go to my MRI, then to dinner with Jacob, Hudson, and my parents. I don't have my results yet, but I'm anxious and kind of shocked. I've never had a real injury.

That night, I keep my knee elevated. But based on the pain, I know this isn't normal. I know it's bad news.

I'M WITH MY TEAM when I get the MRI results. I've completely torn my ACL. I've torn my meniscus, too, and the bones in my knee are bruised from smacking together when my ACL tore in half, which is what's causing the pain. In the locker room, I break down and cry. I've come back from so much—from Dick, from pregnancy, from Arik's death, from the drama with Tara, Nicole, and Amy. This feels so unfair. I'm supposed to be in my comeback era, not my downfall one.

There's a BYU basketball game that night. The college's main orthopedic surgeon is working there. My trainer wants to get me operated on as soon as possible. He has Lauren take me through the team's tunnels to meet with the surgeon while the game is going on. The doctor has me sit on a table and starts yanking my knee around. It's so painful I feel nauseous.

Later, one of my teammates asks if I'm going to try to play senior year. She says she wouldn't. "I'd be done," she says, sitting on the blue-carpeted floor.

I understand where she's coming from. But I've just started playing well again. I've just gotten my groove back. I want one more shot.

"I'm coming back," I say.

I'm too competitive to quit now. And I've come too far. I owe it to myself to see how good I can be. And I want Hudson to know that he can do anything he sets his mind to.

FIFTY-THREE

LAUREN NEEDS TO CHECK IF I CAN TAKE A REDSHIRT SEAson. The logistics are complicated, since I've already played multiple preseason matches. She sits in her office, bent over her desktop, counting the matches I've played.

At first the NCAA says I played too much. It's not going to work for me to redshirt. Lauren tells the NCAA they counted incorrectly. She's adamant. She spends hours advocating for me. In the end, I make it by one day. If that's not a sign, I don't know what is.

IF I GET SURGERY through BYU, it's free. But my parents want me to see the best person if I'm going to be competing on the tennis court in ten months. My mom finds a surgeon who takes care of the Olympic ski team. He's the only surgeon in the area who does a hamstring graft as opposed to a cadaver or a patellar tendon. He has a long waitlist, but he loves BYU, so he gets me in for a consult right away, then schedules the surgery for a month later, once the swelling has gone down.

When I go into the operating room, I stare at the word "Yes," written in Sharpie on the knee he's going to be slicing into. The tools are terrifying, the air freezing. Jacob's skipped school to be with me. I lie back on the table and take deep breaths. *One day*, I tell myself.

AFTER SURGERY, MY LEG is bandaged from my hip to my toes. I wear a compression sleeve and a brace to prevent clotting. I can't get out of bed. Hudson is scared of me. He cries when he sees me wearing my brace. It breaks my heart.

My mom is sleeping in my room with me because I can't move on my own. She helps me use the bathroom, take a shower, everything. The surgeon's given me pain medication, but I stop taking it after a couple days. I'm afraid of getting addicted.

It's a relief to start physical therapy, because at least that feels like moving forward. I go to a clinic in Provo, but after a couple weeks, Lauren and I decide I'm not making enough progress. She talks to the football trainers, who say they'll work with me. I start working out with them two and a half hours a day, five days a week.

It's incredibly painful. At every appointment, they loosen the crank on my brace so I can bend my leg a little more. The first exercise I do involves letting my knee hang off a table. It sounds simple to let it dangle there for ten minutes, but it hurts so much that I sweat. Next, I try to bend my knee. I don't get on a bike for a few weeks. Once I do, I pedal so slowly it doesn't seem fair to call what I'm doing exercise, but I know I need to do it.

ACL RECOVERY IS LONG. I've never seen a college tennis player tear theirs and come back at the same level. They usually end up playing doubles or last in the lineup. I know I want to come back at number one. I want it so bad. But I'm impatient. I start to get depressed. I just want something to go my way. I want a win instead of these constant setbacks.

IN MARCH, I GO to a party. It's my first night out since surgery. I hobble around on crutches talking to people, thrilled to be out of the house. Jacob thinks I'm flirting with other guys.

He gets angry and leaves, then he comes back to get me because he's my ride. He's a good boyfriend. He worries about me even when he's mad.

We drive back to Lauren's house, where he stares into the pine trees. I wonder if he's going to break up with me. Instead, he says, "I feel like you don't love me." I do love him, but I'm tired—of being injured, of having to be the comeback kid, of being a single mom. And grief and trauma still sometimes hit me in waves. I don't say anything. "Do I not make you happy?" he asks.

"You do," I tell him. "I'm just in a bad place."

FIFTY-FOUR

THINGS GET BETTER OVER THE SUMMER. JACOB AND I GO to Europe with my family. Exploring together makes us fall even more in love. My parents make us sleep in separate rooms, but they don't need to. Jacob and I both know we want to wait until we're sealed in the temple to have sex.

Back in Southern California, Jacob and I see each other most days, but it's still not enough. I know Jacob is thinking about proposing. I'm nervous, but I also can't wait. I'm sure he's the one. I'm ready to make it official. I'm ready to become a real family.

In July, I go to Utah for Presley's fourth birthday. Jacob stays in San Diego, where he's selling pest control again. The day after the party, I wake up to three missed calls from him. He never calls multiple times. I have a bad feeling. I sit up and call him back. His voice sounds off when he answers. Shaky. He tells me he's had a bad day. I'm like, *OK, we all have bad days, what's really going on?* He keeps talking. He tells me that he drove to the temple, parked his car, and prayed about when we should get married.

"God didn't give me any answers," he says.

I can hear Lauren, Presley, and Hudson playing in the living room. I press the phone to my ear and walk outside the house, where I sit on Lauren and Kirk's front steps.

Jacob tells me how frustrated he feels. "If I can't take care of myself, how am I going to take care of a family?" he asks. "What if God is telling me to go on mission?"

I start crying. I feel confused and betrayed. I thought we'd handled the mission question months ago. I understand how much pressure there is for men to go on mission. But this conversation feels like going backwards. Maybe Jacob's path is different from the rest of his family's. To me, he won't be a lesser person for not going on mission. It's not for me to decide, but I really believe his path is to be a family with me and Hudson.

Jacob says we shouldn't talk for a few days so he can clear his head.

When we hang up, I drop my head into my hands. Jacob is supposed to be the stable one—the one who drops off Kneaders French toast and OJ before I travel, the one who picks me up from the airport with bagels, the one who fights for our relationship, who fights for me. Is he breaking up with me?

I stand up and go inside, where I tell my family that Jacob might go on mission after all. They're shocked and angry. It's not that they don't support people going on mission. In general, they do. My mom has a leadership role in the church, and my dad served for two years in Mexico City. But Jacob had told all of us he wasn't going, and my family hates to see me in pain over a man again. None of us like the whiplash.

LATER THAT DAY, JACOB calls my dad by accident. I'm not in the room when it happens. I just hear about it from both of them afterward. Jacob, who thinks he's calling his stake president at church to talk about going on mission, says, "President Clark?"

My dad is like, "No, this is Marshall."

Jacob is embarrassed, and my dad's upset. He doesn't want to see me get hurt again. He and Jacob stay on the phone for five minutes, talking about Jacob's decision. When my dad hangs up and tells me about the conversation, my whole family thinks it's over. Jacob was talking about getting his papers in order. He sounded sure about going.

Debriefing with my parents and Lauren, I can't stop crying. I know Jacob is the one. I spent months debating dating him, months going back and forth

FIFTY-FIVE

WHEN I GET BACK TO CALIFORNIA A COUPLE DAYS LATER, Jacob and I break up. I'm expecting it, but it still takes my breath away. One afternoon, we're talking in my parked car near his grandmother's house in Aliso Viejo, and I feel like he's hearing me—like he knows that his grandmother, his dad, and his brother are in his ear; that he's confusing his family's voices and insecurities for God's; that he needs to follow his heart and do what *he* wants to do instead of listening to what his family wants for him.

But the next evening, we're in another car—his, this time—sitting in my parents' driveway, and he tells me he's going on mission. It's done. Official.

I can't believe it. The thought of starting over and having one of those, "So, what do you like to do for fun?" conversations devastates me. I walk into the house, go straight upstairs, crawl into my parents' bed, and sob. I feel like a little kid.

My mom rubs my back.

My dad says, "Right person, wrong time."

I nod and keep crying. Hudson took his first steps out of Jacob's arms. He calls him "Dad." How could it be over between us? How is it that even possible?

IN THE MORNING, MY dad tells me it doesn't have to be all or nothing. We're sitting in the kitchen. "You can still date Jacob," he says. I've already erased all the photos of us from my Instagram. "Try," my dad continues. "Date him until he leaves." He's frustrated with Jacob, too, but he respects the fact that he wants to go on mission. "There's a middle ground here, Mayc."

I don't usually hear my dad, especially when it comes to boys. I didn't when he told me to break up with Dick before starting BYU, or to break up with Dick during BYU, or to break up with Arik. But I do this time. I get up from the table and call Jacob and tell him I want to talk.

He skips work and comes over.

When Hudson sees him, he says, "Dada!"

Jacob cries, hugs Hudson, and says, "This feels so right." I agree. It does.

JACOB AND I SPEND the rest of the summer together. There are only three weeks left at this point. Almost every day, we go back and forth on the mission topic. He asks if I'll wait for him while he's on mission. I say no. I'm a mom. If he leaves, I'll date. I'm not going to put my life—or Hudson's—on pause for anyone.

Jacob flip-flops on his decision, saying he'll stay. But the next night, he goes back to his parents' place, hears them out, and tells me he's going to go on mission after all. I'm exhausted by the back-and-forth, and so is he. If he really wanted to go on mission for himself, I'd support him. But this decision feels like the result of people-pleasing.

One night, I cry to Jacob and say, "I don't know why nothing can ever be perfect for me. I feel like I'll never get my happily ever after." Jacob hugs me but can't promise anything. Sobbing into his neck, I try to remember that my life is so much better than I thought it would be. But I want more. I want to be married to him. I want to be a family.

JACOB AND I START opening up to each other more. He tells me how inadequate he feels about not having gone on mission. If he doesn't go, he's not sure if he can be a respectable man and father. He's the only man in his family to not serve. His dad went to Colombia. His brother went to Missouri.

And all his cousins on his dad's side went as well. Will he be a failure if he doesn't go too? Will he always wonder about the what-ifs?

I tell him about Dick. I've talked about the abuse before, but one night, when we're sitting in my car outside a movie theater, I confess almost everything. I don't say what happened the night Dick assaulted me in his car. I haven't told anyone what happened after that—to this day, not even my therapist knows the details. But I talk about how trapped I felt with him, how scared I was, how wrenching it was to not be able to turn to anyone for help because of the blackmail. We cry together.

It feels good to share more with Jacob. I realize that for months, I'd been keeping him at a distance. Now that he might leave, I give myself over to him.

This is good for our relationship. We're both softer with each other. And I start to see Jacob looking at me and Hudson differently. He's talking about us as his forever. I wonder, as summer ends, if his mind is starting to change.

It is. In August, Jacob and I are sitting in a car again, and he tells me he's going to do one more semester at BYU, meaning he's not going on mission after all; he's going back to school. He says it so nonchalantly. My first thought is: *I know.* But I wonder if he really means it. He's had so many changes of heart about mission.

What if it happens again? Then what?

FIFTY-SIX

MY PARENTS BUY A HOUSE IN UTAH. IT'S TOO CHAOTIC for Lauren and Kirk to have me, Hudson, and my mom staying with them now that they have two little kids.

I like the new place. It's a ten-minute drive from Lauren and Kirk's house, so we still get to see them all the time. And Hudson has his own room now, with a crib and white walls. When Jacob sleeps over, he stays on the floor of Hudson's room on a blow-up mattress. I sleep in the queen-size bed one room over. I spend a lot of time wondering when Jacob's going to propose. We're not talking about the mission at all anymore, but I won't feel settled until we're engaged. In the back of my head, I wonder if he is going to change his mind again and bail on me and Hudson. I tell myself that if Jacob doesn't propose by the end of the year, I'll break up with him.

In November, a friend of a friend DMs me asking if I want to pose for a stylized engagement shoot. I ask Jacob if he'll come with me. He doesn't seem that excited about it, but he agrees. The day of the shoot, Jacob says Hudson should come with us too. I'm worried this is going to annoy the photographer. Hudson is a toddler—he's not the best photo subject. But Jacob really wants him there, so I agree.

On the drive to Provo Canyon, I wonder briefly if this is a setup. Is Jacob proposing? Is the photographer in on it? Jacob won't stop smiling, which makes me suspicious. I try to keep my expectations in check, but the idea of getting engaged to Jacob makes me giddy. I've wanted it for months now. It's hard to believe it might actually be happening.

When we get out of the car, the wind is gusting. It whips my hair into my face and makes Hudson's eyes sting. We walk up the canyon, where Jacob lays out a picnic blanket, and we start posing for photos. The images can't be good. Hudson won't sit still. The wind is blowing a thousand miles an hour. My eyes are literally running. I check Jacob's pockets for a ring, but don't see one. I feel slightly disappointed, but at the same time relieved. It's cold and gloomy out. Hudson's hanging on by a thread.

The photographer suggests that Jacob and I sit on the picnic blanket we've brought from home with Hudson. She hands Jacob a book and says, "I thought it would be cute if you read this to Hudson for some of the pictures." He passes it to me.

The first couple pages are cute but generic. I don't realize it's about me and Jacob until the sixth page, when there's a paragraph describing exactly how I like my popcorn. I look at Jacob, my heart pounding, and turn the page, reading, "Now it's time for your Happily Ever After." I tear up, remembering crying to Jacob in the car about how I would never have my happily ever after. Here it is, after so much hardship, so many mistakes, so much heartbreak.

Jacob stands and helps me up. I can't believe this is happening. I feel like I'm in shock as he kneels and proposes, Hudson holding the book, the wind blowing the yellow grass behind us. Everything is perfect. I'm so happy I can't stop crying.

Afterward, our families meet us at a restaurant in Provo to celebrate. Looking around the table, I feel at peace. After all the arguments and all the back-and-forth, everyone finally seems aligned. Jacob and I are getting married. We're a family.

FIFTY-SEVEN

I DON'T GET TO REVEL IN THE ENGAGEMENT FOR LONG. I need to continue rehabbing my knee. I'm still not supposed to run, but I can play tennis if Lauren hits directly to me.

By December, I'm allowed to jog toward the ball. A few days after that, I'm allowed to lunge. My new knee feels sketchy, like it could snap again at any moment. I try to trust it.

Soon, I'm doing strength training in the morning, a private tennis lesson in the afternoon, and then practice with the team, meaning I'm exercising five hours a day. It's hard, but after weeks of being unable to put pressure on my leg or even let my foot touch the ground, it feels amazing to move my body again. And I want that number one spot back.

Except Lauren's brought in a girl from Russia she says is really good. Anastasia. She's six feet tall and speaks with a thick accent. When she says, "Focus," it sounds like, "Fuck this."

Despite the fact that Anastasia is my competition for the number one spot, I like her right away. When we play off at practice, I realize Lauren was right: Anastasia is seriously talented. She hits hard. And her height puts her at an advantage. Still, I win. I'm too competitive to let that number one spot slip out of my hands.

Afterward, I think about our assistant coach's tattoo. It says, "Rise from the Ashes." My teammates and I have made fun of him for it for over a year, but one afternoon, when it's hot out and he's wearing a tank top that shows the entire thing, I ask him what it means. He tells me he played tennis for the University of Utah, but his coach didn't believe in him. He wouldn't even put him in the lineup. So he transferred from the University of Utah to the University of Nevada in Las Vegas, where he became the number one player and beat Utah. I love that he kept fighting and rose up. It's how I feel about my life too. Later, when we're at our team retreat, he tells a group of us that he thought about leaving the team after I tore my ACL. He only stayed because I had been through so much and he admired my grit. I feel my throat tighten, realizing I influenced him as much as he influenced me.

FIFTY-EIGHT

DAN, THE OLDER GUY WHO CALLED ME OUT OF THE BLUE during my junior year, is still texting me. I tell him I'm engaged. He says that since I'm not married in the temple, Jacob and I aren't sealed together for eternity, which means I'm still technically available.

"I'd really love to meet you and give this a try," he writes.

I ignore him. But his text triggers me.

A few weeks later, when I'm driving back from the airport after dropping my mom off for a flight, a song comes on that reminds me of Dick. Without thinking, I start speeding. When I look down, I see that I'm going over 100 miles per hour. I'm driving like Dick. It's like I don't care what happens to me. I slow down, my chest heaving, my knuckles white on the steering wheel. I'm terrified. It's the first time I've thought about hurting myself since I was pregnant with Hudson.

A few days later, at tennis practice, Lauren sees that I'm upset. She pulls me aside and reminds me there are resources available if I'm having a hard time. She knows our parents don't believe in therapy. But she's learned about a therapist who's available for BYU athletes to help with trauma. "I know you don't really share your feelings," she tells me, both of us standing outside her office. "But if you want an outlet that's not family, I can connect you to someone who I think can help you."

I'm hesitant to go. I don't love the idea of therapy. But I usually listen to

Lauren, so I try to keep an open mind. And I imagine what might've happened if I'd driven 100 miles per hour into the nearest wall.

A WEEK LATER, I'M sitting across from a therapist named Tom in the BYU Counseling and Psychological Services Center. Tom is kind. He has pink cheeks. He's bald. He sits in a rolling chair in front of a computer while I take the blue couch.

It's weird to tell someone at BYU what happened, after sacrificing so much to keep it all a secret. The Mayci from freshman year would've died before telling a BYU employee that she drank, or smoked, or had sex. But Tom makes me feel like I can trust him. He's the first person who tells me I was raped. He says it simply, facing me and pronouncing the words slowly and calmly. Hearing it makes me feel like a weight is being lifted off my chest. His reaction is so different from the bishop's. He believes me.

I START TO SEE Tom regularly. He helps me see that I was a kid when Dick raped me—that the trauma I've experienced was Dick's fault, not mine. That I need to stop blaming myself. It helps, but I still struggle with hating myself for allowing what happened to continue for so long.

During one of our sessions, I ask him when I should tell Hudson about Arik. He tells me that it's best to tell kids hard things between the ages of three and five, meaning it's too early for me to tell Hudson about Arik now.

It's nice to have a plan going forward. Everything feels less out of control.

THAT SPRING, I TRY to balance therapy, wedding planning, tennis, and school.

On senior day, I play my last match at BYU. I want to win for Lauren and for myself. Kirk has gotten a job in California. The plan is for Lauren to finish out the season, then move to Orange County with her kids. The idea of being in Utah without her is bittersweet. We've gone through so much together—both on and off the court. But she's never loved Utah, and there's been so much drama with the tennis team. I understand her wanting to leave.

My doubles match goes well. Anastasia and I play together and win. But in singles, I lose the first set 4–6. I battle back and win the second, meaning I need to take the third. Anastasia is playing a singles match next to me. If either one of us loses, our team does too. Both teams crowd the sidelines and cheer. Everyone's screaming.

I'm down three match points. One court over, Anastasia is fighting hard. Each time a point ends, we're slow to serve. Neither one of us wants to mess up and end the day for the team. I win my next point. So does Anastasia.

When she wins her match, it's all on me. My match goes to a tiebreaker. It's as close as it can be. When I win 7–4, I scream. It's the most rewarding match I've ever played.

My team rushes onto the court, shouting and hugging me. Lauren and I both cry. It's the end of a long and challenging journey for both of us. As I press my face into her shoulder, I can't help but wonder how my tennis career might have looked if I hadn't faced so many hurdles. I try not to dwell on the what-ifs, but it's hard not to imagine where I would be as a tennis player if I hadn't been raped, or gotten pregnant, or lost Arik, or torn my ACL. Would I be gearing up to play professionally?

I look up at Hudson in the stands and wonder: Would I even want that?

FIFTY-NINE

ON MY WEDDING DAY, I WAKE UP WITH A COLD. SITTING up in bed, my head pounding and nose running, I feel ready to start my life with Jacob. I shower, then start getting ready for the day. I'm at a hotel with a group of friends and my sisters, who are my matrons of honor. I didn't ask them if they wanted to take on that role. They just told me they were doing it, which is the story of my life. I don't mind. It feels right—another day as the baby of the family.

Once I'm dressed, Lauren takes me to a cliff in La Jolla, where Jacob and I do our "first look." I'm nervous pulling up, but when I get out of the car and Jacob turns around to see me as his bride for the first time, I feel safe and perfect and blessed.

Afterward, Jacob and I get sealed in the temple, then we do a second ceremony at our reception venue. We want to make sure Hudson and the other people who weren't allowed into the temple get to see us get married.

The bishop who had told me everything with Dick was my fault is there—my parents felt like they had to invite him—and I pretend not to see him.

I take Jacob's hands and tell him that he made me feel confident that my situation as a young mom was normal. "You accepted Hudson as if he were your own from day one," I say at the altar. "I could not have imagined a better person for me and especially Hudson."

MAYCI NEELEY

JACOB AND I SPEND our wedding night at the Ritz. I have a vision for how the evening is going to go. I'll come out in white lingerie and a silky robe untied and stun Jacob, who'll be sitting on the bed. Neither of us will be sweaty from dancing or from our two ceremonies.

This isn't Jacob's vision. We've been dating for two years and are finally going to have sex. He tells me that if I'm going to insist on showering, we're going to shower together.

"No way," I say, laughing.

I leave him on the bed and go into the bathroom alone. I need the scene of me coming out in my lingerie. I need the presentation. I've literally thought about this moment since I was a teenager.

SIXTY

THERE'S NO HONEYMOON. JACOB IS SELLING PEST CONtrol for the summer again, this time in Texas. There's a better market there than in California, and Jacob and I need the money. We're both still students: I have one semester left at BYU, and he still needs to complete BYU's finance program. Plus, we'll need to pay rent and for childcare come September, now that we're married and my mom won't be helping with Hudson anymore.

I've saved a lot from my scholarship checks, but I'm worried about money. My parents have a rule where they don't financially support their kids once they're no longer single. And I don't expect them to. But I underestimate how big the adjustment to married life will be.

In Texas, Jacob and I know almost nobody. He works Monday to Saturday from eight in the morning until nine thirty at night, so we almost never see each other. And I don't know how to fill my days as the sole childcare provider. It's too hot for Hudson to play outside: the first time he goes to the park, he burns his butt on the slide. And the apartment the pest-control company sets us up in has a roach problem—ironic. Hudson, who's two, kills them, which is good, because I hate them. But he can't do anything about the smell of cigarettes that lingers in every room. I try to take him outside to avoid it, but because of the heat, our options are limited. We go to the mall because it's one of the only places with air-conditioning, and we visit my sister McCall, who's in Dallas for her husband's work. Our kids are twelve days apart, and it's nice that they can play together. But I still feel isolated. I miss my friends in Utah. And I miss Jacob.

When he isn't too busy, we get together for lunch, which means a thirty- or forty-minute drive each way. We meet on the side of the road wherever he's door-knocking. Sitting with him and Hudson in the car eating Torchy's Tacos or Chick-fil-A is my favorite part of the day. I just want to be with my family.

But I spend most of my time trying to wrangle a toddler in 110-degree heat and figure out who I am and what I want to do with my life. I've stopped working out, because now that I'm done with tennis, I'm like, *What's the point?* But without the structure, I feel listless. Plus, I'm on birth control for the first time, which I don't like. Jacob and I know we're not in a financial position to bring another kid into the world, but the pill makes me anxious and uncomfortable. I feel moody. I gain weight, which makes me feel slightly self-conscious. Plus, now that I've been sealed in the temple, I've started wearing garments. People who aren't Mormon like to call these "magic underwear." I don't understand how you're supposed to hide them under your clothes. I wear one dress over and over again, because it's baggy, with narrow blue and white stripes and cap sleeves.

The best thing about Texas is that there's an end date. I count down the days until we go back to Provo, and I spend a lot of time thinking about what I want to do once I graduate BYU in December. I always assumed I'd be a stay-at-home mom, but I learn, in Texas, that I need something else to do. Something to make me feel fulfilled. I've worked too hard in school to waste my education. And when I hear McCall's friends talk about their days dropping off their kids at school and going to Target, it depresses me. I want a career. I just have this feeling that one day I'll be successful—one day, I won't be living in an apartment filled with roaches. One day, I'll be someone.

Maybe, I think, I should share my story. I don't want to become an influencer. I don't even have two thousand followers on Instagram. But I want to help people who are facing the same challenges I faced. I want that little black diary my dad gave me to become something. I don't know what I'm doing with my life, but thinking about starting a blog makes me feel a little less lost.

TOLD YOU SO

I BUY A USED camera and learn how it works. When Hudson is happily playing, I fiddle with the camera's settings and watch YouTube videos about lighting, retouching, and framing. I download Lightroom so I can do even more photo editing. It costs $20 a month, which feels like a lot of money. Still, it's worth it. I know if I'm going to share my story on the internet, I need to have photos accompanying it. And they need to look good.

Drafting the beginning of my blog is thrilling. My family doesn't know most of what happened with Dick, and at first, I think about omitting it entirely. But I was such a Goody Two-shoes before I met him. My story wouldn't make sense for readers if I don't explain how he changed me. I have to put it all out there. I hope that maybe it can help someone else who's going through an abusive relationship.

Once I have some words down and a few dozen photos, I start setting up a website. During Hudson's naps, I listen to podcasts about WordPress. None of this is my zone of genius. This is my zone of incompetence.

But when I buy maycij.com I feel proud of myself. I'm starting something.

And when it's time to go back to Utah, I almost feel grateful for my time in Dallas. It was hot and hard and lonely. But it reminded me who I want to be.

SIXTY-ONE

MY DAD WALKS THREE AND A HALF MILES EVERY MORNing. He does the same loop around our neighborhood in Coto de Caza. In September, when I'm back in Utah for my last semester of BYU, he calls me from the stoop of our house. He's read part one of my blog, which I posted the night before. He's proud of me, but he's upset about what I went through. "I wish I'd known about all of this," he says. "I wish you'd told me."

"You would've made me come back to California."

"That's probably true," he says. I can picture him grimacing in front of his house, his elbows on his knees. "You know," he continues, "we should see if there's a way you can help people and monetize this at the same time." I laugh. My dad's motto has always been "Don't Get Screwed." It's so like him to already be business-minded.

But I appreciate his thinking. I've already decided to post on my Instagram every Sunday to let my followers know that a new part of the blog is going up.

Over the course of six months, my following grows from two thousand to ten thousand. People start to post about my writing. They comment saying other people need to read my story. I get hundreds of DMs from women who say my story helped them. It's overwhelming. But simultaneously, it makes me feel like I've found my purpose. I start to understand that the hardships I've suffered have put me in a place where I can help others.

Almost all the feedback I get is positive. But one Sunday, a couple weeks after my first blog post goes up, I get a DM from Dick's sister: the one I called when he ran after me with scissors and I had to hide in that hockey boy's closet.

She writes, "Mayci, I just read your blog post and I am so so fucking disappointed, saddened, and enraged by the things you said." She says what I published could ruin Dick and send him to jail. "I get it," she writes. "You guys had some crazy fights and times but you were also part of it."

I don't respond. Her whole family is in denial about how Dick abused me, mainly because they don't really know anything about what actually happened. I don't need them to hear me or to understand my side of the story. I just need to speak my truth. I'm sick of people trying to silence me. Dick did that for way too long. It's time for me to share my experience. That's how I'm going to move forward and feel free.

A COUPLE MONTHS AFTER the message from Dick's sister, I hear from a burner account that accuses me of lying on my blog. "Stop trying to act like you were a true single mom, your parents paid for everything, your mom took Hudson for months at a time, or came to Utah and helped out with him," the sender writes.

I know my financial situation can be confusing for people. My family has money. I'm privileged, and I know it. But I haven't just been handed things. When I was a single parent, I didn't expect my mom to buy me formula or diapers. I used my scholarship money and the checks I got from WIC. And I've always felt guilty that my mom gave up so much to watch Hudson when other single parents don't get that kind of support.

JACOB AND I ARE still worried about money. We're supporting our family while we're both finishing school, which is stressful. We're spending $1,600 a month on random babysitters, and the costs feel like they keep coming. Gas. Food. Textbooks. Rent. But I really want a new camera lens. I decide to buy one as an investment, and to keep talking to my dad about advertising on the blog and on Instagram. I get serious about learning how to monetize my growing social media platform. I like it. Plus, taking myself seriously as a content creator helps me remember that haters come with the territory.

IN OCTOBER, I GET invited to my first influencer event. It's a local movie premiere for a film that never makes it to theaters. I can't believe I've gotten invited. I still don't have that many Instagram followers, but my engagement is good.

For the premiere, Jacob wears black jeans, a blue button-down, and black boots. I'm in a black dress and nude heels. Hair middle-parted and down.

When I excitedly tell my dad about it later, he reminds me to stay kind, to not change. He tells me that even though people are following my story, it could end tomorrow. I know that.

Except good things keep happening. In November, I get my first brand deal. A company wants me to take pictures in their boots. I'm like, *Why not?* Jacob and I go up to Sundance, where I take hundreds of photos. The company has asked for twenty. I want to go above and beyond, so I naïvely give them fifty that they can use royalty-free forever. I don't understand the business behind any of this yet.

A couple months later, a reality-TV producer reaches out saying she's read my blog and wants to talk about doing a show about my family. I've never wanted to do reality TV. I've never been interested in being famous. All I've ever wanted is to be able to support myself and my family. But I'm at the beginning of my career and open to any opportunity. I take a bunch of calls with the producer. My parents and sisters do too. I learn that there are a lot of steps before you film a pilot. My parents and McCall have reservations about a show, but we've always called my mom the Kris Jenner of tennis, and Lauren and I love to joke about how a show about tennis moms could give *Dance Moms* a run for its money. Why not go for it?

WHEN I FINALLY GRADUATE from BYU in December, it's anticlimactic. I won't get to walk until spring, and since I've been interning at a digital marketing agency called Fusion 360 in Salt Lake City already, joining the workforce full-time doesn't seem like a huge transition. Still, I'm excited to start my job there.

The biggest downside is that now that I'm working full-time, I have even less time to spend with Hudson. Jacob finds us a nanny. I'm so low-paid that we can't afford to offer as much as she deserves, so we tell her to take Hudson whenever she wants: to get her nails done, or to see her friends, or to the mall.

On weekdays, I commute to work, listening to podcasts about influencing on the drive. After work, I grab fast food and commute home, listening to more podcasts. I'm absolutely obsessed with learning how to turn social media into a real business. I don't have many people in Utah anymore. Lauren and Kirk are gone. Taylah has moved. My mom is back in California. I'm too busy to make new friends.

On the weekends, I spend all my time with Hudson. I feel terrible about how little I see him during the week. I don't work out. And Jacob and I go on maybe one date every four months. I'm totally focused on Hudson, work, and social media. I'm hustling. And besides, we really don't have any extra money to spend on dates. Things are tight.

SIXTY-TWO

A YEAR AFTER MY BLOG GOES UP, I GET A DM FROM DICK'S ex. She asks if he's the abuser I talked about on my blog. I say yes, and she tells me that she experienced a lot of the same psychological abuse and manipulation I described online. She tells me Dick would follow her to her job because he thought she was getting hit on. Talking to her, I feel a lot of validation. She reminds me that I'm not alone. I tell her she isn't either.

Later, when I get another DM asking if the guy who abused me is Dick, I respond, "Yes." The person writes back saying their friend is engaged to him. I say, "Just so you know, his ex-girlfriend before me said similar things to the stuff I wrote. It's not just me." I feel terrified for Dick's fiancée. I want her to be careful. But other than telling my story and having her friend warn her about him, there's nothing I can do.

JACOB AND I ARE doing really well, but I still sometimes get triggered from the trauma with Dick. Jacob and I will be messing around and I'll freeze, or I'll realize while we're kissing that I have my arms pressed across my chest. I get flashbacks of times Dick assaulted me. One night, Jacob asks if I'm not attracted to him. I tell him I am, which is true, and explain that I just get triggered sometimes. It's the first time I'm fully honest with him about how the sexual abuse continues to affect me. I had thought it would just go away on its own, but it hasn't.

Jacob responds perfectly. He's totally understanding and kind. Together, we learn that it's better for me to have sex when it's not super dark, and that too much foreplay is actually triggering because it reminds me of Dick. It's never been easy for me to be vulnerable. But opening up to Jacob, even when it's painful and awkward, helps both of us.

THE LONGER I'M AT Fusion 360, the more I wonder if it's what I really want to be doing. I've gotten close with a coworker named Cassidy, who's been teaching me about videography and editing. And I'm still learning a lot about social media. But I want to do something bigger. In the corporate world, someone is always determining my worth, and I resent it. I know pretty quickly that I'm not going to climb the ladder fast enough. I know I'm going to do something on my own.

But until that happens, I have to grind it out, which means spending nine hours a day away from Hudson. I feel like a bad mom when I get home and he cries and clings to me. And it's exhausting to juggle my job, housework, the videography I'm doing as a side hustle, and the blog. When Cassidy switches to part-time to go to film school, I decide it's time for me to do more too.

Online, I see that Goldman Sachs is hiring. In my first interview, a hiring manager tells me that working as a social media operations specialist isn't a creative role. That's OK. I want to try something new. I go through three more phone interviews. I'm glad the hiring process is done on the phone and not in person, because ever since someone at Fusion 360 told me I got the job because I'm pretty and blond, I've been self-conscious about my worth.

The reality TV show has fallen through—I never learn exactly why, but it seems like the producer was let go or demoted. I'm OK with that. But I really want the Goldman Sachs job, and I scream when I get it. This will be a big pay jump for me and Jacob. We'll be able to afford to go on dates. I'm excited, but some of my favorite memories are the nights where Jacob, Hudson, and I watched movies on a blow-up mattress while eating candy from the dollar store. The money stuff has been stressful, but it's not like we haven't found ways to have fun.

My mom and I shop for business-casual attire at Zara. I'm used to wearing sweats to work. At Goldman Sachs, I can't even wear jeans. I'm excited to be in a business-casual environment. I feel like a big girl. My parents are happy that I'm happy, but they don't really care about the job itself. They want to know when Jacob is going to start making real money. All the pressure to have a career is on him, not me. That's the traditional way things are done in the Mormon church and in Mormon society.

It's frustrating to feel like my professional achievement isn't taken seriously, and I resent the traditional gender roles I grew up with. Why can't I be the breadwinner? At Goldman Sachs, my boss's boss is my age and incredible. She holds her own in every meeting. She takes herself so seriously. I've never been good at that, and I try to learn from her. It seems so much easier to be firm and authoritative as a man. I worry that every time I set a boundary, I seem like a bitch. Growing up, there were so many I-told-you-so's. So many times my family members said I'm the baby and that I should listen to them because they know better. At Goldman Sachs, I try to trust myself to make the right decisions. Everything I learn there—about competitor analysis, loans, deposits, and even myself—is captivating.

A COUPLE MONTHS AFTER I start at Goldman Sachs, Jacob and I sit Hudson down on the couch. It's time to tell him about Arik. I think about what my therapist at BYU had said: that kids between three and five are best able to process the information that their parent isn't related to them biologically. I take out my phone and show Hudson a picture of me at the hospital. "See how Mommy is alone?" I ask. Hudson isn't particularly interested in the picture. "Look," I say. "Daddy isn't here."

Hudson glances at Jacob, who says, "I didn't get to be there when you were born." Hudson nods. "See how I'm not in the photo? I met Mommy later."

I show Hudson a picture of me and Jacob at BYU.

Jacob explains that Hudson had a different daddy, who died. He tells him that this means Hudson has two dads. Jacob makes it sound like a really positive thing. What kid wouldn't want two dads?

"Do you have any questions about any of this?" I ask.

Hudson doesn't. He's totally happy to get the news, but also eager to get back to playing with Legos. Jacob and I let him go, then look at each other on the couch, relieved.

SIXTY-THREE

JACOB AND I START TALKING ABOUT HAVING ANOTHER KID. We don't want too big of an age gap between Hudson and his little sibling, and since we know we're going to need to do IVF for genetic reasons, it seems like we should start the process, since we have no idea how long it'll take. I'm privileged to have good insurance through my job, which means we can almost afford it. We know it will still be challenging, but I don't think either of us expects it to be so hard.

The first hurdle is finding a good clinic. Jacob and I don't really know what we're looking for, so we find one that's popular in Utah. Going into the process, I'm afraid of the shots. I hate needles. I assume injecting myself with hormones will be the worst part.

But I quickly learn that what's actually hard are the unknowns. Jacob and I have no idea how long IVF will take. We don't even know if it'll work. And even with my benefits from Goldman Sachs, it costs a huge amount of money, so there's this massive financial burden you're taking on without any guaranteed success.

My first appointment is easy enough: a check to see how many follicles I have. Next is the saline ultrasound. Using a catheter, the doctor shoots saline into my cervix while I have my feet in stirrups. The girl who does the procedure literally wears a headlamp while she's rooting around down there.

Afterward, Jacob and I get bad news. There are polyps on my uterus that

I might need to get surgically removed. I feel scared—of the surgery, of the shots, of the wait after my eggs and Jacob's sperm are combined, of the genetic testing. Half the embryos people make won't last more than five days. What if none of ours do?

And I feel a little like a fraud. When you tell people you're doing IVF, everyone assumes it's because you can't get pregnant, but there are so many other good reasons to do it, many of them private and personal. Even though I plan to document the experience on social media, I don't want to have to tell my twelve thousand followers exactly why Jacob and I are doing IVF. I share so much of my life already. Jacob and I want this to be private. Still, I want to be honest, especially if it helps other people going through similar things. It's a complicated balance. I decide to film the process but post the videos in the future in case something goes wrong. I set up my camera when Jacob gives me shots every morning at six a.m. I film some of the blood draws, too, but I get them so often I don't tape them all.

MY INSURANCE SAYS THEY'LL cover $30,000 of the process. At first, we think that should be more than enough, especially because IVF meds alone typically cost around $7,000.

But there are all these hidden costs. It's incredibly frustrating. I don't understand how the fertility pharmacies get away with charging people so much more than the stated price. The whole thing is unethical. One night, when I'm feeling frustrated, I download TikTok. I don't really understand it, but I like scrolling through the videos, and occasionally, Cassidy and I send each other funny ones. It's a nice way to stay connected now that we don't work together anymore.

Over the next couple weeks, while I'm feeling anxious about the IVF process and unable to read about egg retrievals and statistics anymore, I upload silly videos for fun. I'm starting to imagine making a living as a content creator, but not on TikTok. I'm focused on Instagram. I don't really get TikTok. And I have no following there.

A few weeks later, I'm sitting in bed, mentally preparing myself for my egg retrieval, when I hear the sound of someone throwing up. It's Jacob. He has a stomach bug. I assume this means my surgery is off. I won't be able to go under anesthesia if I get sick. For three days, I sanitize the entire house. I literally shiver each time I hear the sound of Jacob throwing up upstairs. Empty boxes of Clorox wipes pile up in the garage. I hate the idea of having to reschedule my appointment. And I've had a phobia of throwing up since I was a little kid.

The day of the surgery, I make Jacob wear a mask and keep his distance. We get to the clinic thirty minutes early. The anesthesiologist is cocky; he gives me something to relax. Jacob leaves the room, I pass out, and the next thing I know, the anesthesiologist is walking me down the hall to recovery. My stomach hurts. It feels like I got repeatedly punched in the gut.

After ten minutes, the doctor comes in and sits across from me. He says we got nine eggs. My brain can't process that. I've heard about women getting thirty or forty. I was expecting at least twenty, and so was he.

I say, "Nineteen?"

"Nine," he says.

"What happened?"

He doesn't have an answer. I feel exhausted and scared. Because Jacob and I are doing IVF for genetic reasons, we know some of the embryos won't be viable. We're both worried we're going to have drained our savings for nothing. I go home, where I scroll through IVF message boards online. Other women all say the shots made them feel horrible. I haven't loved them, but I haven't felt that bad, either, and I wonder if I haven't taken enough meds. I feel defeated. The shots, the blood draws, the time, the money—it was all for nothing.

The next day, I go to work with a heating pack pressed against my stomach. I'm sitting at my desk when I get a call. Two out of the nine eggs are dead.

I get another call later that day: five of the remaining seven eggs have been fertilized. Now we have to wait to see if any of those will make it to the blastocyst stage. It's agony. But after a few days, we hear from the clinic that one has made it and two more might. In the end, they both do, and all three are sent off for genetic testing, which will take two weeks. I count down the days. I can't imagine doing this process all over again. I can't imagine the waiting, or the shots, or finding another $30,000.

audience. I decide to keep posting. Maybe TikTok will become the new Instagram. Plus, I'm stuck at home and bored, and I love making videos. So why not share them?

By May, I'm putting up two videos a day. It's a good distraction from the lockdown and from waiting for my transfer. And my follower count keeps growing.

I start making friends through TikTok. That's where I get in touch with Mikayla, who's also posting about being a mom in Utah. I see her videos and think she seems sweet. And I want more mom friends! I'm mostly hanging out with people who don't have kids.

The first time Mikayla and I meet in person, she's so quiet and standoffish that I wonder if she hates me. But we become real friends almost immediately after that. We make gingerbread houses and watch *The Bachelor* and talk about juggling work, family, and TikTok. Mikayla is the best. I absolutely love her.

AT THE END OF May, I do my transfer. When I take a pregnancy test five days later, it's positive. After all the money, the worry, and the oil progesterone injections that needed to be heated and left bruises all over my butt, Jacob and I are having a baby. IVF worked.

I yell for him to come upstairs and look at the test, and then I cry. This feels so different from the two pregnancy tests I took in college. Hugging Jacob in our bathroom, the test on the counter, I feel for that girl who sobbed for hours in the dark shower, convinced her life was over. I wish I could go back in time to show her this moment. Everything is coming together. I have a husband, I'm pregnant with my second baby, I like my job, and I'm helping people through my social media. I'm incredibly grateful.

A COUPLE WEEKS LATER, Jacob makes pasta for dinner. It looks gross. I eat it anyway, then sit on the air vent to help with my nausea while I finish work. I have bad cramps. I hunch over my laptop, while Jacob takes Hudson to the park. At some point, I go upstairs to pee. I'm on my way back down when I feel something wet. I assume it's the suppository I've had to take as part of the IVF treatments, but I stick a finger into my underwear to make sure. When I pull it out, it's red and dripping.

Alone on the stairs, I scream, "Fuck."

I call Jacob, then our nanny. She comes over so Jacob and I can go to the emergency room. While we wait for an ultrasound, I'm terrified I'm miscarrying; that Jacob and I are going to lose our baby. Our one healthy embryo.

When I finally get a vaginal ultrasound, Jacob and I see a heartbeat. The anxiety isn't gone, but it's better.

I go to the IVF clinic the next day to make sure my HCG levels are rising. They are, but I get put on pelvic rest. No biking. No sex. Nothing strenuous. When I get my next ultrasound, the tech finds a hematoma. It's big—bigger than the sac the baby is in. But it's in the best possible spot. An inch to the right or the left, and I would've miscarried.

I try not to obsess about it. I still feel worried, but I remember that my body is meant to carry a baby. I think about drinking when I was pregnant with Hudson, and taking steroids for my injured labrum. That pregnancy turned out fine. I tell myself this one will too.

SIXTY-FIVE

WHEN I GET A LITTLE FURTHER ALONG IN MY PREGNANCY, I decide I want a nice stroller: the Nuna. I become fixated on it. I'm convinced it'll make my life perfect. I email the brand multiple times. Nobody from Nuna responds. I keep trying. Eventually, I get in touch with someone there, and we go back and forth. They don't seem particularly interested in me until I tell them I have a TikTok with two hundred thousand followers. I tell them I'll post about them, and they send me a stroller and a car seat in exchange for being featured in three videos. A feature is way easier than an ad. I don't really have to do anything other than tag them.

Jacob and I celebrate the Nuna deal by grabbing pizza from our favorite place. Those car seats and strollers are expensive, and we still don't have a lot of money. This is a big win for us. I feel like I've manifested something.

As my pregnancy progresses, I get more offers. Hostess reaches out to me. So does a grocery brand. Most of these deals are for less than a thousand dollars. The brands still don't seem to fully understand TikTok's reach.

But I start making good money as an influencer. It's not enough to quit Goldman Sachs, which I like anyway. It's certainly not enough to support a growing family. But for someone who used to be on food stamps, it's something.

A COUPLE MONTHS LATER, I find out my baby, whom we've named Harlow, is breech. I really want a v-bac (vaginal birth after cesarean). I want that experience of having a vaginal birth, which I didn't get with Hudson, but Harlow won't budge. To cheer me up, Jacob says we should look at houses together. We've never had a conversation about buying our own place, but suddenly we're serious about it. We drive around and talk about if we want to pull the trigger or not.

Six weeks later, Harlow is born via C-section. Giving birth with a partner is magical. I've never been so in love with Jacob. He helps me get into the shower at the hospital, changes every one of Harlow's diapers, makes sure I have enough food and water, and asks the nurses to teach him how to swaddle. He's the perfect newborn daddy. I'm so grateful.

When we get home, he's the one who notes Harlow's poops and pees and how often she eats. He's the one who protects my space.

I DIDN'T HAVE POSTPARTUM anxiety after Hudson. I was just so relieved to have him by my side. To get to love him. To know God was done testing me.

But with Harlow, it's harder. When my parents leave Utah after her birth, I lose it. I start crying and can't stop. Jacob calls my mom because he's so worried about me.

AS THE WEEKS GO on, my anxiety gets worse. I do everything I can to hide it, but I'm overcome by panic attacks multiple times a day. I convince myself I have brain cancer, that Hudson's going to be hurt in a school shooting, that Harlow will stop breathing in her sleep. My stomach always hurts. I lose too much weight. I'm skinnier than I was in high school. This makes me even more worried. I'm convinced there's something really wrong with me; that I'm going to die and leave Jacob behind with two kids. I look forward to the end of each day, just so I can go to bed and not have to feel this way.

It's funny, because on paper, my life is the best it's ever been. I've overcome all these struggles. I have a husband I love, a growing career, two beautiful kids, friends who make me feel seen—even my dream stroller. But my anxiety makes me miserable. I feel like, any second, I'm going to lose everything. Maybe it's because I've seen people die too young and know it can happen in an instant. I become terrified my life will fall apart.

When I was training for tennis and would get tired while sprinting on the treadmill, I'd speed it up instead of slowing down. My instinct has always been to push myself harder when I'm closest to my breaking point. That's how I approach my life postpartum. I throw myself into parenting, work, and my TikTok, which is still growing. I hope, if I'm busy enough, the anxiety will just go away.

IT DOESN'T, BUT WHEN Harlow is two months old, I make a video about my life story. I know before I post it that it's going to go viral. There are certain videos that I know will strike a chord—usually the ones that make me cry while I'm editing. This one gets over 20 million views—the most I've ever gotten.

That week, three managers reach out to me. Jacob and I take the meetings together. Each of these managers tell me I am going to be something. The one I sign with, Danielle, says that my lifelong dream to write a book is not just possible, but that it will happen with time. I like that she assumes the sale. That's the kind of confidence I want on my team.

I'm still working full-time at Goldman Sachs. I'm breastfeeding Harlow, too, which means I'm pumping at work. Twice a day, I sit in the pumping room, each time for thirty minutes. It's not enough. Most days, my boobs ache. I need to pump for a third time before driving home, but I can't bear to be away from Hudson and Harlow for an extra half hour. Plus, I'm starting to make more money from social media than I do at my job. Even though I really like and appreciate Goldman Sachs, I decide I want to go somewhere a little chiller. So I find a job at New U Life as a marketing manager. I tell myself I'm going to use the job to focus on influencing and managing my anxiety. Maybe, by working from home more, I'll be able to relax. I'll be able to settle into a routine as a parent of two kids who shares her life online.

SIXTY-SIX

I'M STANDING IN A ROOM SURROUNDED BY WOMEN IN Santa Claus–themed lingerie. My beige sweater dress, which I thought was appropriate for the Christmas girls' night my realtor's girlfriend invited me to, makes me feel matronly and out of place.

Across the room, Taylor, whom I've been following on TikTok for two years but never met in person, is drinking and posting about wanting to kiss girls on her TikTok Live. She doesn't seem that interested in meeting me.

I make eye contact with her and say, "Hi!" She smiles at me. I tell her we've been following each other on social media for a while.

She's like, "Oh, we have? What's your name?"

It's awkward. Miranda, whom I've also never met in person, is drinking too, but she seems nice and normal. We talk for a while. She says I should come make videos with her and Taylor. I don't know if I'm hot enough to do their content. I mostly post about being a mom, and I definitely don't wear crop tops anymore.

"Oh yeah that would be fun," I say, looking back over at Taylor.

Miranda says she wants to film a TikTok right now. All the girls at the party are down. I borrow a red dress, and then Miranda gets everyone together—all the lingerie Santa Clauses, plus me in my borrowed dress—and she asks us to do something sexy. I'm like, *What is sexy?* I've spent the last six months anxious that I have literal brain cancer. I run my arm down the stairs while everyone else grinds on each other. I'm so embarrassed. But also, I realize, I'm having fun.

Afterward, I give Taylor and Miranda a ride home. They're both drunk. In the car, they tell me they want to go out to the bars later, but their husbands are going to stay home. I think that's a little strange, but I tell them I'm down to do more TikTok content with them. Why not? I already have 1.2 million followers, but I feel like this is a good opportunity to collaborate and grow even more. We decide to get together and film for a day in January.

A couple days before we film, Miranda tells me I should wear a white crop top and black yoga pants to her house for the MomTok content day. I don't own a white crop top. I have a white sports bra, but I've just stopped breastfeeding, so my boobs are tiny. I can't show them off on camera. I decide to wear a white cropped jacket over the bra. It might look stupid, but at least I won't be practically naked. It's still the most skin I've shown since sophomore year of college.

I tell my boss at New U Life that I'll be offline for a couple hours, then drive to Miranda's house. Filming takes hours. The idea is each person gets one video. When we're done, I try to linger after and talk to everyone. I think it would be nice to be friends with the other moms. But for everyone else, it seems like this is just business.

When I post my TikTok video afterward, Mikayla messages me and says, "Are you cheating on me?" She's not actually mad. I tell her I'll invite her next time. She can join MomTok too.

MOMTOK MAKES ME MORE confident. My anxiety still flares up sometimes, and I'll find myself checking Harlow's breathing or panicking about a headache, but it trends better. It helps that I've stopped breastfeeding. It feels like my hormones are regulating.

The initial awkwardness I felt around Taylor and Miranda starts to fade too. I find that spending time with these women helps me feel hot and fun and remember a part of myself that I lost when I got pregnant unexpectedly at nineteen.

But my overall views go down. MomTok is clearly not good for my personal brand. I still film with the girls because I think the dip in engagement might be temporary, and I can tell MomTok is going to be something. I even tell my manager, Danielle, about it.

I say, "This could be a reality show."

Danielle tells me she's already looking into it.

A couple months later, Taylor and I are at a spin class together. I've been trying to hang one-on-one with all of the MomTok girls to get to know them better. I like Taylor a lot now. She's edgy and fun.

After class, when we're both covered in sweat, Taylor tells me she's gotten too many TikTok penalties and her account has been banned. Her manager has been working on it, but it's already been a week.

"Who's your manager?" I ask. Her account should absolutely be back online already. Plus, she has a million more followers than I do, but isn't making more money than me. She tells me who her manager is, and I give her Danielle's info instead. Taylor signs with her, and Danielle has her account back up in a day. I'm happy to help. I like MomTok, even though it's continued to make my engagement drop, and I really do want to be more connected with the other moms in the group. Mikayla, Whitney, and I are actually close, but everyone else, except sometimes Taylor, remains more of an acquaintance than a friend.

SIXTY-SEVEN

IN JANUARY, MIRANDA'S HUSBAND INVITES ME AND JACOB to come to a cabin in Big Bear for the weekend with "about six other couples." He says some people will be drinking and some people won't. I tell him I don't know if our nanny is free for the weekend, but I'll see if we can swing it. I know she'll be free, but I don't want to commit.

In the morning, I wait for Miranda to text me. I assume her husband has told her we're invited, but I want to make sure she's OK with the idea of us coming too.

She doesn't text me. After a couple hours, I reach out to her and say her husband invited us. Should we bring our ski clothes? She responds saying the group probably isn't going to be doing any skiing or tubing. They'll be chilling in the cabin.

That means partying. Miranda also says Jacob and I might have to sleep on the couch or share a room with another couple, even though her husband told me the cabin sleeps thirty-eight. I realize she doesn't want us to go. I say our nanny isn't free after all. But I start to wonder if something weird is going on with that group.

I KEEP THINKING ABOUT it. In February, Taylor posts a video of herself wearing a lingerie top and jeans with some friends and their husbands. It stands out to me. Maybe I'd wear that top at a Galentine's Day event or to a party in college, but I wouldn't wear it out with my friends' husbands.

I have Mikayla, Whitney, and a couple girls over to my house for a girls' night and tell them I have a theory that Taylor and Miranda are swingers.

I don't want them to share it with anyone else, because I'm not interested in starting rumors. But I feel like it's strange that Taylor is throwing these college-style parties with select girls from MomTok. There must be something else going on.

THERE IS. FIRST IT seems like Taylor had an affair. Then it looks like a lot of the women in MomTok are swinging. I tell Jacob about the news as it comes. It's quite the scandal. We're entertained by it, and also a little shocked. I truly thought the only people who swung were couples over forty going through midlife crises.

One night, we go to Texas Roadhouse as a family. It's Hudson's favorite restaurant. He pounds rolls as I read Reddit posts about MomTok aloud. I feel bad being on my phone at dinner while Jacob is wrangling both kids, but I'm addicted to the tea. It's crazy to read rumors about people you know. I can't get enough of it.

A couple days later, Jacob's sister messages him and asks if he and I are good. She wants to make sure we weren't involved in the swinging scandal.

He's like, "Mayci and I have nothing to do with this. Don't worry."

Jacob and I don't care that much about public perception, which is good, because there's a lot of judgment around the swinging scandal. I keep my chin up in church and around Utah. My take is people can think what they want, but I know who I am and I know what I do. This is nothing compared to what I've been through, and I know better than to let judgy people get under my skin.

My uncle reaches out next. He's seen my face in the news coverage about the swinging scandal. He asks my dad if I'm a part of it. My dad tells him not to worry, that I wasn't involved in any of it.

I'm lucky my parents don't care about the rumors. Our family doesn't care what other people think of us. We know what we do and who we are. Outside opinions don't matter. And that's a good thing. I'm pretty sure that if I did care what people think, I wouldn't have made it out of 2015.

A COUPLE WEEKS AFTER the swinging scandal breaks, Miranda invites me, Mikayla, and Whitney over to explain what happened. Even as Miranda's talking to us, Whitney can tell that Miranda is lying. Afterward, Whitney voice-memos me and Mikayla and says, "I don't believe a word she's saying." I always give people the benefit of the doubt. I don't see why Miranda would have invited us over to lie to our faces. But Whitney is sure, and she's convincing. She texts Taylor and says we all want to see her to hear her side of the story.

I've been in touch with Taylor since the swinging drama, mostly because everyone else has been turning their backs on her and I've felt like she has no one in her corner.

Taylor comes over to my house and tells me, Whitney, and Mikayla everything. It contradicts what Miranda told us.

"I have no reason to lie to you," Taylor says, leaning against the counter in my kitchen. I believe her. I don't hate Miranda for lying to me, but I don't understand why she did. She could've just as easily said it was personal, that she didn't want to share anything.

When we're done talking, the four of us want to do what we do best . . . film a TikTok.

There's a trend where people go to the car wash and spray themselves and their cars with the hoses. We decide to try it for fun. We change into spandex shorts and white shirts, then drive down the hill in my car. When we get to the car wash, we grab hoses and start blasting each other with colorful soap and water, each of us taking turns to climb onto the roof of my car.

I don't think I've ever had this much fun filming a TikTok. To this day, I have dents in my hood. They're absolutely worth it. No part of that day felt like work.

SIXTY-EIGHT

MY BOSS AT NEW LIFE U ASKS IF I'M INTERESTED IN starting a business together. He has a ton of experience in the supplement industry, and we see eye to eye on pretty much everything. We have a series of meetings where we talk about the fact that I wanted better gummy prenatal supplements when I was going through my own motherhood journeys.

When I leave New Life U a couple months later to work as an influencer full-time, we start Babymama: a natal vitamin line. I'm really excited about the idea of cofounding Babymama—I've always wondered why there aren't more specific vitamins to take postpartum, or while you're trying to conceive—but starting any business is a huge risk. And we know we don't want to take investor money, which means I'll need to invest some of my own.

While we're working on getting Babymama off the ground, I decide to go back to therapy: EMDR this time, because I've heard it can help people heal from trauma, and because I've continued to struggle with my mental health, especially after leaving my job at Goldman. I'm pretty sure focusing on influencing is the right thing, but it was incredibly reassuring to have a regular salary, and ever since the news about the swinging scandal came out,

MomTok has blown up. It was weird even before then—Mikayla and I had even talked about leaving the group—but now it feels like it might be over. I'm not sure what that will mean for me. Now that Jacob and I are living in our new house on his salary and my social media money, we're stretched thin. There are a lot of moving parts. I'm relieved to have someone to talk to.

My EMDR therapist is named Heidi. During our sessions, she sits in a leather chair beside a computer. I take the couch. I'm supposed to close my eyes and think about a traumatic event while she buzzes me with different frequencies. We use a stack of cards to help me come to different conclusions. They all have sentences on them. One reads, "I did something wrong." Another says, "I am not worthy."

Heidi asks me to pull whatever card resonates with the situation I'm talking about. I keep coming back to "I can't forgive myself."

Through EMDR, I learn that I did the best I could for myself with the knowledge I had at the time. I shouldn't hold my nineteen-year-old self to the standards I now hold myself to at twenty-seven. It's similar to what Tom allowed me to see at BYU.

I'M SITTING ON MY porch in Utah when my manager texts me to say that a reality show about MomTok is happening. Things have been so weird since the swinging scandal. It feels good to have something exciting happen. I scream, then call Mikayla. We're both thrilled, but also nervous because neither of us has really pictured exposing our lives on reality TV. Still, we've been talking about this for a long time. It's a big win.

I START FILMING THE pilot for *The Secret Lives of Mormon Wives* at the end of September.

The first scene I film is at a coffee shop with Taylor. I'm surprised by how little instruction there is. The crew just hooks me up to a microphone and then the cameras roll. Both Taylor and I are overly smiley. It's neither of our personalities, but it's so weird and exciting to be filmed that we can't help feeling nervous.

The cameras are a lot closer than I expected. I'm like, *How's my hair? What if there's something in my teeth?* But after ten minutes, I start to feel like being filmed is no big deal.

SIXTY-NINE

JACOB AND I TALK ABOUT HAVING A THIRD KID. WE GO TO Orange County to work with a different IVF clinic. I didn't love the one we used in Utah. I still think I should've gotten more than nine eggs. I pitch the clinic, and we agree to a trade: they'll give me free treatment (minus the fertility medicine and genetic testing) in exchange for me posting about the experience.

A couple days after my first appointment in Orange County, I take Harlow with me to pick up Thai takeout. She's wiggly, and I'm exhausted and stressed from thinking about beginning the IVF process again. While I wait for our food, I feel someone looking at me. I scan the room and make eye contact with Dick's parents. He's sitting in a booth with them. I feel hot. Sweaty. Dick's face is angled away from me, like he's hiding. I don't know what to do. I don't want him to see me and Harlow. But my food isn't ready. I peer into the kitchen and try to shush Harlow.

When I get our takeout, I hurry outside and climb into my car, sobbing. Seeing Dick feels like my worst nightmare. We haven't spoken to each other in eight years.

On the drive home, I think about the therapy I've done, and the fact that Dick was hiding from me too. He was scared to show his face. I'm in control. Not him.

A COUPLE DAYS LATER, Taylor gets arrested, and filming is put on hold. I'm antsy. I never set out to do reality TV, but now that it's happening, I've started slacking on my TikTok and Instagram. My manager reminds me that I can't rely on the show. I need to keep working with brands and producing content. But it's hard and stressful. I miss having a regular income and benefits from a full-time job. Working on Babymama is exciting, but it's also incredibly stressful. My mental health still isn't perfect. Jacob and I are unsure when to do our embryo transfer. And as much as I love being with Hudson and Harlow, parenting is work. On top of it all, Jacob has been laid off along with 20 percent of his company, so I have the added stress of being the sole financial provider. There's just so much up in the air.

During this time, I get updates on the show every once in a while. When we're finally greenlit, I'm so excited. We're actually going to film a reality show. It's really happening.

JACOB TAKES MY CAR on the first day of filming, leaving me my grandpa's 1995 truck we bought one year earlier because I was feeling sentimental when he died. The steering wheel is crooked, and the Dodge logo is at an angle. I video myself in the driver's seat, a literal set of drawers in the truck bed behind me that Jacob forgot to take out. It's the White Turd all over again.

I like shooting the season, but it's busy. I film almost every day from January through March.

It's a relief to wrap, just because I get my time back, but it's also destabilizing to go from filming almost every day to nothing. I start feeling depressed again. None of us knows if the show is going to be a hit. Jacob hasn't been working for over a year, which means it's on me to keep the lights on, put food on our table, and pay for everything else. Babymama has finally launched, but it's not an overnight success. I feel the weight of the world on my shoulders. I'm nowhere close to hitting my career goals for the year. And I feel like Jacob has stumbled on his career path because he's been focused on helping me with mine. Everything has been go, go, go, and now it's too slow again. What if all my success was a flash in the pan? I remember my dad telling me not to take anything for granted. I don't think I have, but Jacob and I have a mortgage, and we haven't made enough money for me to feel comfortable. I wonder if I've stretched our family too thin.

Jacob and I are still planning to have another kid. But I don't feel like I'm mentally or financially in a place where I can transfer an embryo. We've been talking about holding off, and we decide that's the right thing to do. We need to wait until things stabilize.

THE HULU TRAILER COMES out in August. Everyone panics except me and my parents. They're like, *Who cares?* They know I don't drink, swing, or party. Maybe I don't wear my garments enough. And maybe I swear a little more than the average Mormon, and drink the occasional iced mocha. It's nothing to get up in arms about.

Two days after the trailer is released, the Church of Latter-day Saints releases a statement calling out "recent productions" that "depict lifestyles blatantly inconsistent with the teachings of the Church." There are tons of articles about this, but it all feels like a lot of fuss over nothing. Most people in our lives and the church are pretty much OK with it. When my parents' bishop asks my mom if she's on the show, she tells him that she's filmed some scenes. He's young and relaxed. He's not too worried, and they move on to talking about members who need support. It's not an issue.

And even if it were, I wouldn't care. I'm over living my life worried about what church members might think. It's my life and I'm not doing anything wrong. I'm active in the church, I pay my tithing, I hold a temple recommend—meaning I follow all the guidelines that allow me to enter the temple—and I teach five-year-olds about Jesus.

I'm just ready for the show to come out. I feel like I've been waiting so long for it. And because I'm not allowed to post any TikToks I film with the girls until the show airs, I'm taking a financial hit. I have to hope the show makes my following grow so I can get more brand deals when it airs. It sometimes feels like I've been working hard to have to work hard again in the future. And occasionally, I feel a little like the show has taken over my life.

MAYCI NEELEY

AT LEAST THE PREMIERES are fun. The first one, in L.A., is more of an influencer party. Hulu flies all of us and our partners to California, where they put us up in a nice five-star hotel. Show travel doesn't always feel fancy. But this time, it's like a vacation. We all drive down Sunset Boulevard, where we see a billboard with our faces on it. I can't believe it. When I was in L.A. with some of the girls the year before, we talked about whether we'd be up there. Now it's actually happened. The same billboard and everything.

I'm excited, but I have no idea if this is actually going to change my life. The thought of it makes me super anxious. My life isn't always easy, but I love it. And I love my privacy. I'm worried how the show will affect my kids. Will it make things weird at school? I tell myself I probably should've thought this through before committing to a reality show, and that it's too late to second-guess my choices now. I should just sit back and be open to whatever happens next.

A couple days later, the cast organizes a second premiere in Utah. Hulu sends signage and posters, but Jessi is the one who actually reaches out to a big theater in the area and asks if they'll show the pilot. We all want to watch it together.

We get vendors to contribute and invite our family and friends. I bring my mom, who stress-eats popcorn the whole time—especially during that scene with me and Taylor talking about my sex life at the start. (I was trying to talk to her about how it's better for me to initiate sex so I don't get triggered. My sex life is great!)

Mostly, the show goes over well. The only issue, if you can even call it that, is that the swearing isn't bleeped out. Some of the girls are pissed. I'm not worried. I only say the F word once, when Whitney walks into Mikayla's birthday party and we're all shocked.

Afterward, Taylor and I fly to New York together to do more press. That entire trip is a "pinch me" moment. We fly first class and have our own five-star mini suites. It's surreal. The night I get in, I take a shower, order room service, and watch a show. Before I got pregnant with Hudson, I imagined myself living in a big city like New York or London. Lying in bed with my room service, looking out at the skyline, I almost feel like I'm living a dream that I'd had for a past life. I never thought I'd be here. I'm so grateful I start to tear up.

SEVENTY

JACOB AND I ARE READY TO DO OUR EMBRYO TRANSFER. The show films it. I'm not nervous about having a producer and a cameraman in the room with me and Jacob. I feel at peace; I know it's going to work. I let the show film my injections too. They also film the day I take a pregnancy test, and my first heartbeat ultrasound.

That morning, in mid-December, I go to the doctor wearing black sweatpants and my black Babymama sweatshirt. My hair is middle-parted and down. Jessi's just tightened my extensions, so naturally I have a dull headache.

I sit in the car while Jacob checks in. It's not like I think I'm super famous, I just don't want to get recognized at the OB-GYN. I don't want anyone to leak my pregnancy. I want to be able to announce it myself when I am ready.

When I go into the doctor's office, I try not to feel anxious. Each time I feel worried that something is going to go wrong—whenever I see an Instagram post about a stillbirth, or talk to a friend about miscarriages, or remember how heartbroken I was to get only nine eggs during my first round of IVF—I redirect my thoughts. I don't let myself worry that I'm going to start bleeding. Instead, I recognize the thought, then remind myself that my body is healthy. That it was made to carry this baby.

I meet my producer and the cameraman in the room, then lie back on a paper sheet on the bed. I want Jacob to take a video of my ultrasound. He accidentally films his face instead of the ultrasound machine. He still gets nervous filming in public and taking up space like that. It's cute.

And the video is sweet: Jacob stares at the screen, not moving, and then his face breaks into a huge smile when he sees the heartbeat. There's instant relief there. Our baby.

The doctor wipes off my stomach and hands me a printout of the image. I say bye to the producer and cameraman, then carry the photo toward the lab, where I need to have my blood drawn.

When I go into the waiting room, I see other women. I quickly pass Jacob the picture, and he shoves it into his pocket. Later, when we're home, he'll pull it out and realize it's crumpled, then use the *Book of Mormon* to flatten it on the table Harlow has covered in Play-Doh. But for now, he just makes sure it's hidden.

While I'm waiting to get my blood drawn, one of the women in the room recognizes me. She's nice. Friendly. She leans over and says she "has to say hi."

I say hi back, then tell her I'm just getting my regular bloodwork done so she doesn't speculate about why I'm there. It's strange to be hiding another pregnancy, this time for entirely different reasons.

Sitting beside Jacob in the waiting room, I try to take it all in. I'm not that lonely twenty-year-old in her childhood bedroom anymore, terrified of how she's going to raise a baby alone. I'm not that twenty-three-year-old married woman, exhausted and guilty about having to spend ten hours a day away from her toddler. I have a career, and a family, and a role on a show where I can wear my scars proudly. I think of the version myself on that cruise ship, so depressed I contemplated jumping into the ocean.

I'm so grateful that when the lab calls my name, I can stand and say, "I'm here."

ACKNOWLEDGMENTS

THIS BOOK HAS BEEN MY DREAM FOR MORE THAN TEN years. It wouldn't have been possible without the help of so many people.

My editor Ian Straus has been extraordinary throughout this process. I knew from the moment I met him that I wanted him to be a part of my book writing journey. I'm so grateful to him for his editorial eye and guidance, Rachelle Mandik for the wonderful copyedits, Lindsey Stewart for the cover shoot, and Margaret Southard, Julia Prosser, Hannah Bishop, and everyone else at Simon & Schuster for making my dream a reality.

Danielle Pistotnik believed in me from day one and has helped me make my wildest passions come true.

Cait Hoyt, Gaby Sheiner, and everyone at CAA have been beyond incredible. Thank you for everything you've done for me and for this book.

This memoir would've been impossible without the work of Ally Glass-Katz. Thank you so much for your help shaping and sharing my story.

My dad gave me the journal that started all of this and told me—when I was at my lowest—to write everything down because one day it could help someone else. My mom supported me through every one of Hudson's prenatal appointments, took care of him while I went back to school, and has always been there for everyone in our family.

Both my parents have always believed in me and opened up avenues to achieve my goals and for that—and everything else—I'll be forever grateful.

ACKNOWLEDGMENTS

Lauren and Kirk, who helped me so much as a single mom and still support me in more ways than I can even thank them for.

McCall and Alex, who I love so much and so deeply appreciate.

Tom Holmoe, Trevor Wilson, Vern Heperi, Tom Golightly, Robert Walz, Fui Vakapuna, and all the others at BYU who helped me through physical therapy, my classes, and treated me with love and compassion—thank you.

Arik's whole family, thank you so much for supporting me as I share my story. I am grateful for your love and acceptance of me and my family.

Arik, I know you can't possibly be reading this but losing you impacted me so much more than anyone will ever know. Your story has inspired so many people around the world and I don't think I would be writing this book without you.

And my friends—thank you for being there for me during the highs and the lows. I love you all.

Jacob, when I met you, I knew you were special. Thank you for doing so much at home while I've been filming, running Babymama, and working on this memoir. I and the kids are so incredibly lucky to have you and we love you so much.

Hudson, Harlow, and the baby girl in my belly—you are my world. By the time you're allowed to read this, I hope it inspires you to know that you can accomplish anything you set your minds to. Your trials only make you stronger and your mistakes do not define your future. I love you so much.

And to you, the reader. This is the book I needed ten years ago when I was at my lowest. Things will get better. I promise.